Chickens

Chickens

Tending a Small-Scale Flock for Pleasure and Profit

BY SUE WEAVER

HOBBY
H F
FARM
PRESS™

An Imprint of BowTie Press®
A Division of BowTie, Inc.
3 Burroughs
Irvine, California, 92618

Karla Austin, *Business Operations Manager*
Nick Clemente, *Special Consultant*
Jarelle S. Stein, *Editor*
Kendra Strey, *Assistant Editor*
Jill Dupont, *Production*
Lisa Barfield, *Book Design Concept*
Allyn A. Salmond, *Book Design and Layout*

Library of Congress Cataloging-in-Publication Data

Weaver, Sue.
Chickens : small-scale chicken keeping for pleasure and profit / Sue Weaver.
p. cm.——(Hobby farms)
Includes bibliographical references.
ISBN 1-931993-48-3
1. Chickens. 2. Chickens–United States. I. Title. II. Series.
    SF487.W378 2005
    636.5–dc22

    2004017010

BowTie Press ®
A Division of BowTie, Inc.
3 Burroughs
Irvine, California 92618

Printed and bound in Singapore

10 9 8 7 6 5 4 3 2

Table of Contents

Why Chickens?

Seventy years ago, throughout the countryside and in cities large and small, backyard chicken coops were the norm. Chickens furnished table meat and eggs; most everyone kept at least a few hens. Years passed and attitudes shifted; small-scale chicken keeping became gauche. By the end of the twentieth century, while agri-biz egg and meat producers, immigrants, rustics, and aging hippies were keeping chickens, cultivated urban and suburbanites were not!

The times they are a-changin' once again. As our world becomes increasingly frenetic, violent, and stressful, a burgeoning number of Americans are seeking a quieter existence. "We'll move to the country," some decide. "We'll live on a small farm and commute or work from home; we'll garden . . . we'll have chickens!"

Nowadays, from Minneapolis to New Orleans, from Los Angeles to New York City and all points in-between, throngs of city dwellers and suburbanites raise and praise the chicken. A few miles farther out, more hobby farmers are apt to raise chickens than any other farmyard bird or beast. Hens are the critter du jour.

Why keep chickens? For their eggs, of course, and (for those who eat them) their healthier-than-red-meat flesh, whether strictly for your own table or for profit as well. Chickens are easy to care for, and you needn't break the bank to buy, house, and feed them. You may also wish, like many hobby farmers, to keep livestock for fun and relaxation. Surprisingly, chickens make unique, affectionate pets. They offer a link to gentler times; they're good for the soul. It's relaxing (and fascinating) to hunker back and observe them.

This book is meant to educate and entertain rookie and chicken maven alike. Are you with me? Then let's talk chickens!

CHAPTER ONE

Chickens 101

D omestic chickens belong to the Phasianidae family, as do quail, grouse, partridges, pheasants, turkeys, snowcocks, spurfowl, monals, peafowl, and jungle fowl. Domestic chickens are descendants of the Southeast Asian Red Jungle Fowl (*Gallus gallus,* also called *Gallus bankiva*), which emerged as a species nine thousand to ten thousand years ago. Today Red Jungle Fowl have disappeared from most parts of Southeast Asia and the Philippines, but a genetically pure population still exists in measured numbers in the dense jungles of northeastern India. In Latin, *gallus* means "comb," and that is how chickens differ from their Phasianidae cousins. While chickens vary widely in shape and size, all have traits in common, including general physiology, behavior, and level of intelligence.

PHYSIOLOGY

Chickens see in color; their visual acuity is about the same as a human's. While they don't have external ears, they do have external **auditory meatuses** and hear quite well. Their frequency range corresponds to ours. Their smell is poorly developed, and they don't taste sweets. They do, however, easily detect salt in their diets. Other important physiological characteristics to be aware of concern the digestive tract, internal and external structure (bones, muscles, skin, feathers), and sexual characteristics.

DIGESTIVE TRACT

Chickens have no teeth. Instead, whole food moves down the **esophagus** and into the **crop**, a highly expandable storage compartment that allows a chicken to pack away considerable amounts of food at a time. When packed, it's externally visible as a bulge at the base of the neck. Unchewed food trickles from the crop into the bird's **proventriculus**, then to the **ventriculous** (more commonly called the **gizzard**) to be macerated and mixed with gastric juice from the **proventriculus**. It finally passes to the small intestine, where nutrients are absorbed, then to the large intestine where water is extracted. From there it moves to the **cloaca**, the chamber inside the chicken's vent (where its digestive, excretory, and reproductive tracts meet, via the fecal chamber), and finally out the vent. Food processing time for a healthy chicken is roughly three to four hours. Urine (the white component of chicken droppings) also exits the cloaca, but via the **urogenital** chamber.

BONES TO FEATHERS

While chickens have largely lost the ability to fly, some of their bones are hollow (pneumatic) and contain air sacs. Smaller fowl can fly into trees and over fences; when harried, heavy breeds try but usually can't. Chicken muscles are com-

This open-beaked rooster displays his toothless mouth. Since chickens lack teeth, they store food in their expandable crops, where it slowly trickles down to their intestines for proper digestion.

posed of light (white meat) and red (dark meat) fibers. White muscle occurs mainly in the breast; dark muscle occurs in the chicken's legs, thighs, back, and neck. Wings contain both light and dark fibers.

Skin pigmentation varies by breed (it can be yellow, white, or black). Its exact hue is influenced by what an individual bird eats and sometimes by whether a hen is laying eggs. When a yellow-skinned hen begins laying eggs, skin on various body parts bleaches lighter in a given order (vent, eye ring, ear lobe, beak, soles of feet, shanks). When she stops, color returns in the exact reverse order.

Day-old chicks are clothed in fluffy, soft down. They begin growing true feathers within days and are fully feathered in four to six weeks. All genus *Gallus*

Chickens at a Glance

Kingdom: Animala
Phylum: Chordata
Class: Aves
Order: Galliformes
Family: Phasianidae
Genus: *Gallus*
Species: *Gallus domesticus*

Cockfighting

Before chickens, there was the Red Jungle Fowl *(Gallus gallus)*, a flashy, chickenlike bird native to the forests and thickets of Southeast Asia. As a species, it emerged between 6000 and 5000 B.C. By 4000 B.C., *Gallus gallus* was domesticated—not for food, but for cockfighting. By 3200 B.C., high-caste Indian aristocrats were fighting cocks that resemble today's Aseel chickens. Chickens—and cockfighting—spread in the following centuries as traders carried domesticated birds, or chickens, farther and farther throughout the ancient world.

When Egyptian Pharaoh Thutmose III embarked on his 1464 B.C. Asiatic campaign, he was presented with fighting stock as tribute. The first known depiction of domestic fowl—a fighting cock—is etched on a pottery shard of that period. Cockfighting became the rage in Athens about 600 B.C. and was an event at early Olympic games. Greek cockfighters passed the baton to ancient Rome. An avid cocker, Julius Caesar was pleased to find the sport already established in Britain when his army invaded the island in 55 and 54 B.C.

British cockfighting peaked in popularity during the seventeenth century A.D. Every British town boasted a cockpit. Gentlemen breeders held tournaments, often in conjunction with horse race meets. Cockfights were held in manor house drawing rooms, schools, and even in churches. In 1792, the First French Republic took the fighting cock as it emblem; the bird also figured in the design of countless family crests and military standards in France. On the other side of the Atlantic as well, gentlemen, including George Washington, Thomas Jefferson, and Andrew Jackson, raised and fought gamecocks; Benjamin Franklin was a noted referee.

Cockfighting remained a favored British pastime until 1849, when Queen Victoria banned it by royal decree. The sport moved underground, and the average gentleman abandoned his fighting fowl in favor of showing and creating new breeds of exhibition chickens. The movement to ban cockfighting met greater resistance in the United States. While a few progressive states outlawed it as early as 1836, most did not. When asked to support a ban, President Abraham Lincoln is said to have replied, "When two men can enter a ring and beat each other senseless, far be it for me to deny gamecocks the same privilege."

By the end of the twentieth century, the majority of American states had made the practice illegal. There were a few stubborn holdouts. As late as September 2004, cockfighting remained a legal sport in Louisiana and parts of New Mexico.

Today's domestic chickens descended from Red Jungle Fowls, like this sleek modern-day pullet.

birds, including wild jungle fowl, molt (shed their feathers and grow new ones) annually. Chickens molt from midsummer through early autumn, usually a few feathers at a time in a set sequence—head, neck, body, wings, tail—over a twelve- to sixteen-week period. Molting chickens are stressed and can be skittish, moody, and irritable. Molting hens will lay fewer eggs or stop laying altogether.

Sexual Characteristics

Growing chicks generate secondary sexual characteristics—including combs and wattles—between three and eight weeks of age, depending on their breed.

All birds in genus *Gallus*—chickens and jungle fowl—are crowned by fleshy combs and all, except the Silkie, sport a set of dangly wattles under their chins; other Phasianidae do not. Cocks develop larger and brighter-colored combs and wattles than their sisters. At about the same age, cockerels (young male chickens) begin crowing (pathetically at first)

This palm-size Silkie newborn will soon lose his fluffy down. Chicks begin developing feathers within a few days of birth.

and sprout sickle-shaped tail feathers and pointed saddle and back feathers.

Pullets (young female chickens) reach sexual maturity and commence laying at around twenty-four weeks of age. Although female embryos have two ovaries, the right ovary invariably atrophies and only the left matures. A grown hen's reproductive tract consists of a single ovary and a 2-foot oviduct or egg passageway. Her ovary houses a clump of immature yokes waiting to become eggs.

As each matures—about an hour after she lays her previous production—it's released into her oviduct. During the next twenty-five hours, roughly, the egg inches along the **oviduct**, where it may be fertilized, enveloped by egg white (albumen), sheathed in membrane, and sealed in a shell. Because each egg is laid a bit later each day and hens don't care to lay in the evening hours, the hen eventually skips a day and begins a new cycle the following morning. All the eggs laid in a single cycle are considered a clutch.

Behavior

Chickens are easily stressed; stress seriously lowers disease resistance and stressed chickens don't thrive. Panic, rough handling, abrupt changes in routine or flock social order, crowding, extreme heat (especially combined with high humidity), and bitter cold can stress chickens of all ages. Labored breathing, diarrhea, and bizarre behavior are the hallmarks of stressed fowl. To keep stress levels low, it is important that you understand chicken behavior.

PECKING ORDER

While studying the social interactions of chickens, Norwegian naturalist Thorlief Schjelderup-Ebbe coined the phrase "pecking order," now used to describe the social hierarchies of hundreds of species, including humans.

In any flock of chickens, there are birds who peck at other flock members and birds who submit to other flock members. This order creates a hierarchical chain in which each chicken has a place. The rank of the chicken is dependant upon whom he pecks at and whom he submits to. He ranks lower than those he submits to and higher than those who he pecks at.

An angry hen flares her neck hackles to show she's furious. Chickens typically keep to their flocks' pecking orders, which means little infighting, but changes in routine such as relocation or flock additions can result in distressed birds.

A flock of chicks generally has their pecking order up and running by the time they're five to seven weeks old.

Pullets and cockerels maintain separate pecking orders within the same flock, as do hens and adult roosters. Hens automatically accept higher-ranking roosters as superiors, but dominant hens give low-ranking cocks and uppity young cockerels a very hard time.

In a closed flock with an established pecking order, there is very little infighting. Each chicken knows his or her place, and except among some roosters, there is surprisingly little jostling for position. Dominant chickens signal their superiority by raising their heads and tails and glaring at subordinates, who submit by crouching, tilting their heads to one side, and gazing away—or beating a hasty retreat.

The addition of a single newcomer or removal of a high-ranking cock or hen upsets the hierarchy and a great deal of mayhem erupts until a new pecking order evolves. Since brawls are invariably stressful, it's unwise to move birds from coop to coop.

Because low-ranking chickens are shushed away from feed and water by bossier birds, they rarely grow or lay as well as the rest. Indeed, low-ranking individuals sometimes starve. If pecked by their betters until they bleed, they may be cannibalized by the rest of the flock. It's important to provide enough floor space, feeders, and waterers so underlings can avoid the kingpins and survive.

Mating

Like adult roosters, cockerels soon begin strutting, ruffling feathers, and pecking the earth to draw the eyes of nearby hens. This behavior is called displaying. Chicken mating behavior is direct and to the point. The rooster chases the hen or pullet; she crouches when the rooster mounts; insemination occurs. Cocks tread with their sharp toenails and sometimes rake hens with their spurs while mating, occasionally to the point of shredding the poor biddies' backs.

Tidying Themselves Up

When their surroundings permit, chickens are tidy birds. They preen by distrib-uting oil (from a gland located just in front of their tails) over and between their feathers. They also dust bathe. After scratching a shallow depression in suitable earth, they lie in it and kick loose dirt over their bodies, using their feet. A shake of the feathers after dust bathing sets things right.

Chicken IQ

When they founded their show biz animal training business in 1943, operant conditioning (clicker training) pioneers Marian and Keller Breland began by training chickens. Among the couple's first graduates was a chicken who pecked out a tune on a toy piano, another who tap danced

This red hen displays a nearly denuded back, an injury received from a rooster's sharp, spurred feet during breeding.

This handsome light Brahma trio explores the outer fence line of their Missouri home on the farm of Vic and Alita Griggs.

wearing a costume and shoes, and a third who laid wooden eggs to order (any number up to six) from a special nesting box. All were barnyard chickens rescued from a neighbor's stew pot.

With her second husband, Bob Bailey, Marian Breland-Bailey used chickens to teach animal training courses at their Animal Behavior Enterprises in Hot Springs, Arkansas. The couple chose chickens because the birds learn quickly, energetically perform for food, and move at lightning speed. They can easily learn new routines when trainees make mistakes and teach the wrong protocols. Budding trainers honed their reaction times to match those of the Baileys' chickens.

Asked by Animal Action (an Ottawa-based animal rights group) whether he considered chickens and turkeys dumb animals, Ian Duncan, professor of poultry ethnology at the University of Guelph, replied,

Not at all…Turkeys, for example,…possess marked intelligence. This is revealed by such behavior indices as their complex social relationships, and their many different methods of communicating with each other, both visual and vocal. Chickens, as well, are far more intelligent than generally regarded, and possess underestimated cognitive complexity.

A close kin of the chicken, this Royal Palm turkey is a good choice for small farms; the breed is good for meat production for a family and for pest control on the farm.

Chickens are as intelligent as some primates, says Chris Evans, animal behaviorist and professor at Macquarie University in Australia. Chickens understand that recently concealed objects still exist, he explains—a concept even human toddlers can't grasp. Chickens have good memories. "They recognize more than one hundred other chickens and remember them," says Dr. Joy Mench, director of the University of California-Davis Center for Animal Welfare.

Dumb clucks? No, indeed!

CHICKEN CLASSIFICATIONS

Early on, the American Poultry Association (APA) devised a system for classifying chickens by breed, variety, class, and sometimes strain. A breed is a group of birds sharing common physical

Centuries of fine-tuning breeding practices have resulted in beautifully colored birds, such as this rooster found nibbling in the grass.

features such as shape, skin color, number of toes, feathered or non-feathered shanks, and ancestry. A variety is a group within a breed that shares minor differences, such as color, comb type, the presence of a feather beard or muff, and so on. A class is a collection of breeds that originates in the same geographic region.

The APA currently recognizes twelve classes: American, Asiatic, English, Hamburgs, Continental, Mediterranean, Polish, French, Game, Oriental, bantams, and miscellaneous. A strain, when present, is a group within a variety that has been developed by a breeder or organization for a specific purpose, such as improved rapid weight gain and prolific egg production. Chickens may also be classified as light (egg producing) or heavy (meat) breeds or as layers, meat, dual-purpose, or ornamental fowl.

Biological Makeup

Temperature: 103°F–103.5°F

Pulse:
 Roosters: 240–285 beats per minute
 Hens: 310–355 beats per minute

Respiration:
 Roosters: 15–20 breaths per minute
 Hens: 20–35 breaths per minute

Chromosome count: 78

Blood volume: roughly 6% of body weight

Adult body weight: 1–10 lbs.

Natural life span: 10–15 years (pet chickens have lived more than 20)

A Matter of Breeding

Some of today's purebred fowl (chickens whose parents are of the same breed), such as the gamecock breeds, trace their roots to the distant mists of antiquity.

Egypt's elegant Fayoumi dates to before the birth of Christ. Stubby-legged, five-toed Dorkings came to Britain with the Romans. Squirrel-tailed Japanese Chabo bantams, a miniature chicken weighing between one and three pounds, emerged in the seventh century AD Dutch Barnevelders were developed in the 1200s, about the time Venetian merchant Marco Polo wrote of the "fur covered hens" (Silkies) of Cathay. Another Dutch chicken, the deceptively named Hamburg, has existed since the late 1600s and is likely far older than that. The crested fancy fowl we call the Poland was developed even earlier and France's v-combed La Fletche dates to AD 1660. Naked Necks, also called Turkens (possibly the weirdest looking chicken of them all), originated in Transylvania before the 1700s. The first all-American fowl, the Dominique, is an early nineteenth century New England utility fowl.

However, most breeds emerged between 1850 and 1925. Although Queen Victoria's cockfighting ban had already spurred interest in exhibiting chickens, the arrival of the first Asiatic breeds set Britain afire. When Cochins were exhibited at the Birmingham poultry show in 1850, author Lewis Wright gushed, "Every visitor went home to tell of these wonderful fowls, which were big as ostriches and roared like lions, while as gentle as lambs; which could be kept anywhere, even in a garret, and took to petting like tame cats." In 1865, the Poultry Club of Great Britain produced the inaugural edition of its comprehensive *Standard of Excellence*.

America's first major poultry exposition was held November 14, 1849. More than 2,000 birds were shown by 219 exhibitors, and more than 10,000 spectators attended. An *American Standard of Excellence* followed in 1874.

A Dominique pullet appreciates her tasty, new pasture. This first all-American poultry breed first appeared in the 1800s, a time of increasing interest in improving and refining poultry.

Farmer Vic Griggs confines this flock of young light Brahmas to a grower coop. Brahmas are among the few breeds originally recognized in 1874 by the American Poultry Association.

When the APA published its first *Standard of Perfection* in 1874, the only chickens recognized were Barred Plymouth Rocks, light and dark Brahmas, all of the Cochins and Dorkings, a quartet of Single-Comb Leghorns (dark brown, light brown, white, and black), Spanish, Blue Andalusians, all of the Hamburgs, four varieties of Polish (white crested black, nonbearded golden, nonbearded silver, and nonbearded white), Mottled Houdans, Crevecoeurs, La Fleches, all of the modern games, Sultans, Frizzles, and Japanese bantams. In the volume's latest edition, 113 breeds and more than 350 combinations of breeds and varieties are described.

Bantams are one-fifth to one-quarter the size of regular chickens. They come in sized-down versions of most large fowl breeds, although they aren't scale miniatures: their heads, wings, tail, and feather size are disproportionally larger than those of their full-size brethren. A few bantam breeds have no full size counterparts. Besides being cute, bantams can be shown, they make charming pets, and their eggs and bodies, small as they are, make mighty fine eating. The American Poultry Association issues a standard for bantams, as does the American Bantam Association. (These standards don't always agree.)

CHAPTER TWO

Which Chickens Are Best For You?

All chickens aren't created equal. It's important to pick the ones who will meet your needs. There are countless varieties and hundreds of breeds from which to choose. With the passage of time, humans have designed chickens to fulfill every niche: cold hardy chickens, heat resistant chickens, chickens that don't mind being penned up. We haven't designed the perfect chicken—yet! All breeds have certain failings. Furthermore, a breed that would be a bad choice for one chicken keeper (such as hens meant to be confined who can fly out of enclosures) would be perfect for another (as free-ranging chickens, those flying hens would be able to evade dogs).

Before you can settle on the kind of chickens to buy, you need to determine what purpose they will serve and what environment they'll live in. Do you want them for their eggs? Sunday dinner? Feathery companionship? Will they spend most of their time inside or out? Will they have to contend with sweltering summer days or frigid winter nights? All of these factors make a difference in your choice of breed.

Next you must decide whether you want day-old chicks or full-grown birds and how many of them to get. What advantages are there to buying a pullet rather than a chick? Is it better to start with a small flock? If you haven't already done so, you should find out what zoning laws may apply to your keeping chickens as well and how they affect your decision on breed. Do you need quieter birds?
Ask yourself the following types of questions:
• Will your birds be sequestered in a chicken house or do you favor free-range hens? Certain breeds don't like being confined, while others know nothing but.

A cramped coop of ornery Sumatras is a disaster waiting to happen, and find-your-own-feed Cochins might starve.

• How much room do you have to devote to chickens? A few banties can thrive in a doghouse. A dozen 10-pound Jersey Giants? They'll need a heap more space.

• Are there neighbors close by? Squawking, kinetic, freedom-craving, fence-flying breeds likely won't do.

• Are there toddlers in your family? Testy roosters of certain breeds can injure an unwary tot.

• Do winter temperatures plummet below zero where you live? Roos with huge single combs frostbite easily and some breeds simply won't thrive in this type of weather.

• Are you in a region with hot temperatures? Fiery summer heat wilts heavy, soft-feathered breeds like Cochins, Australorps, and Orpingtons, while other breeds take heat more in stride.

• Can you keep your top-knotted, feather-legged friends confined when the weather turns foul? Mud, slush, and fancy-feathered fowl usually don't mix.

Though we can't tell you exactly which breed to buy—describing all the possibilities is beyond the scope of this book—we can offer general advice and name birds that will meet certain criteria. (See chart.) In addition, in the resources section of this book, we list other sources to help you make your decision.

CHICKENS FOR EGGS OR MEAT

Birds with the greatest egg-laying capacity are not the same as those who plump up into the best candidates for the local chicken fry. Still different are the chickens that are the best choice for providing both eggs and meat.

These Leghorns are great egg-layers, but you'll need a covered enclosure since they're among the flying breeds.

Fresh, tasty eggs each morning are just one of the benefits of raising your own birds.

AVIAN EGG MACHINES

If you want eggs—and a whole lot of them—Mediterranean breed chickens are just your thing. Small, squawky, and hyperactive, these birds mature quickly, then everything they eat goes into laying eggs. Undisputed queens of the nesting box are white Leghorns and hybrid layers based on this breed. Other impressive Mediterranean class layers are the Minorca, Ancona, Buttercup, Andalusian, and Spanish White Face.

Some chickens from other classes are laying machines, too. The Campine (Belgium), Fayoumi (Egypt), Lakenvelder (German), and Hamburg (Continental Europe) are popular examples. Like their Mediterranean sisters, they tend to be flighty, specialist hens.

MEAT CHICKENS

Meat chickens—usually White Cornish and White Plymouth Rock hybrids—have broad, meaty breasts, white feathers, and they mature at lightning speed. Broilers (also called fryers) are ready for the freezer in about seven weeks and roasters in just three more.

Be aware that because they're hybrids, these birds don't breed true, meaning their chicks won't possess these stellar features. They also require careful handling because of their abnormally wide breasts and rapid growth patterns, most become crippled as they mature.

DUAL-PURPOSE CHICKENS

Dual-purpose breeds lay fewer eggs than superlayers and mature a heap slower than meat hybrids, but they're

In a typical strutting fashion, this silver-laced Wyandotte rooster makes his dominance known, even on the outskirts of his pasture. The ability to serve as both egg layers and meat producers makes dual-purpose breeds great additions to any hobby farm.

ideal all-around hobby farm birds. They're quieter, gentler, and friendlier than the specialists and hardy and self-reliant to boot. They are broody, meaning hens will set and hatch their own replacements. Nearly all lay handsome brown eggs and are meaty enough to eat, should you wish to do so.

With a few notable exceptions, dual-purpose birds hail from the English and American classes. There are scores of interesting breeds and varieties to choose from.

CHICKENS AS PETS

Do chickens make good pets? Absolutely! They're smart and affectionate, and a chicken costs little to maintain. You can teach your chicken to do tricks—she'll sit on your lap, and she may even sing if she likes you a lot. You don't need a lot of space to keep a chicken. She won't bark at the neighbors while you're at work. You can raise her from a peep for just a few dollars. All in all, a chicken makes a mighty fine friend. Take her along when you run errands; a chicken in your car turns heads!

If pets are your pleasure but you don't plan to handle them, most any sort of fowl will do. If you want pet chickens who are tame, that's another proposition.

Some breeds are rowdy, antisocial, and just not much fun to have around; others are downright cuddly. You want to choose pets from the latter group. Silkies, Cochins, Brahmas, Naked Necks, and Belgian D'Uccles, for example, are easy to tame and make quiet, affectionate, companion chickens. Flighty Leghorns and their ilk can be tamed—but it takes a lot more time and effort.

These chicks have just arrived from the feed store, safely packed in a sturdy, paper towel–lined box. Mail order chicks from hatcheries are typically sold at a minimum of twenty-five chicks per order to provide adequate warmth in the box necessary for a safe arrival.

If you'd like eggs from your pets, that narrows the equation. Not all hens lay scads of eggs. However, most young hens of the generally calm and amiable old-fashioned, dual-purpose breeds crank out one hundred to two hundred (or more) tasty brown cackleberries a year. If a rooster fertilizes their eggs and you allow it, most dual-purpose biddies will hatch chicks. Some ornamental breeds are friendly and lay well, too, but avoid flighty, sometimes pugnacious hybrid super layers and breeds from the Mediterranean class. They don't want to be your friend; they just want to lay eggs. Choose something a tad more laid back.

The best way to bond with a pet chicken is to raise her from a peep, but you can make a grown chicken a pet, too (see box). The vast majority of house chickens are adults the owners originally brought indoors to treat for illness or injury, then made permanent residents because they turned out to be such nice pets.

Make certain that, however you tamed the chicken, other household pets don't look upon your bird as their supper. And be ready to field lots of questions—a big part of having chickens as pets!

BIG BIRD OR CHICKEN LITTLE?

Once you've chosen a breed, you'll have to decide: chicks or full-grown birds? In most cases, the correct answer is chicks. Besides getting the most for your fowl-shopping dollar, you'll know exactly how old they are, and purchased from reliable sources, chicks are nearly always healthy.

THE LITTLE GUYS

Order day-old chicks from commercial or specialty hatcheries. The former sell dozens, sometimes hundreds, of breeds and varieties of quality chicks at modest prices. For most of us, this is the logical way to fly. Specialty hatcheries are run by knowledgeable poultry aficionados who specialize in a specific sort of fowl.

You'll pay more at a specialty hatchery, but if you want to show chickens or to one day breed show-quality fowl, paying extra for specialty hatchery chicks is the way to go. A newly hatched chick can live three days without food and water, subsisting solely on nutrients absorbed from its egg. Therefore, you can purchase chicks from hatcheries on the other side of the country and—shipped overnight air—they should arrive safely at your nearest post office without a hitch. However, sometimes a chick does die in transit. Thus it's wise to order from the closest responsible source, so your chicks needn't travel far-

---

Making a Chicken a Pet

When you brood your next batch of chicks, pick one to hand tame. Carefully pull her out of the brooder for short periods every day. Cup her between your hands, and hold her near your face. Speak gently for a minute or two, then put her back. If you work with her, she'll bond with you. By the time she leaves the brooder, she'll be *your* chick.

To domesticate an older bird, work quietly and carefully. Hold her securely, so she can't flop. Stroke her wattles—chickens like that—and offer her goodies, like bits of fruit or veggies. It won't be long until she's tame!

You might consider training your chicken as a therapy animal; hospitalized children and nursing home residents love to hold chickens. Investigate clicker training, otherwise known as operant conditioning. Widely used to train sea mammals, dogs, and horses, the techniques were originally perfected using chickens!

Which Breed?

Breeds most likely to make great pets
Barnvelder, Belgian d'Uccle, Cochin, Dorking, Jersey Giant, Naked Neck (also called a Turken), Orpington, Polish, Plymouth Rock, Silkie, Sussex

Other easygoing, friendly breeds
Ameraucana, Araucana (usually), Aseel (cocks are aggressive toward one other), Brahma, Dominique, Faverolles, Java, Langshan, Sultan, Welsumer, Wyandotte (usually)

Cold, hardy breeds
Araucana, Ameraucana, Aseel, Australorp, Brahama, Buckeye, Chantecler, Cochin, Dominique, Faverolles, Hamburg, Java, Jersey Giant, Langshan, Old English Game (dubbed), Orpington, Rosecomb, Silkie, Sussex, Welsumer, Wyandotte

Breeds prone to frostbitten combs
Andalusian, Campine, Dorking, Leghorn, New Hampshire Red, New Hampshire White, Rhode Island Red (Roosters are more likely than hens to suffer frostbite; their combs are larger and they don't tuck their heads under their wings while sleeping as hens do.)

Heat-tolerant breeds
Andalusian, Aseel, Brahma, Buttercup, Cubalaya, Fayoumi, Leghorn, Minorca, Modern Game, New Hampshire Red, Rhode Island Red, Rosecomb, Silkie, Spanish White Faced, Sumatra

Flying breeds
Ancona, Andalusian, Campine, Fayoumi, Hamburg, Lavenvelder, Leghorn, Rosecomb, Sebright, nearly all bantams

Noisy breeds
Andalusian, Cornish, Cubalaya, Leghorn, Modern Game, Old English Game

Flighty breeds
Ancona, Andalusian, Buttercup, Fayoumi, Hamburg, La Fleche, Lakenvelder, Leghorn, Minorca, Sebright, Spanish White Faced

Aggressive breeds
Ancona, Aseel (cocks; toward one another), Old English Game, Cornish (cocks), Rhode Island Red (cocks), Cubalaya, Modern Game, Rhode Island Red (some strains), Sumatra, Wyandotte (some strains)

Self-reliant breeds
(good foragers, ideal free-range chickens)
Andalusian, Australorp, Belgian d'Uccle, Buckeye, Buttercup, Campine, Chanteclar, Dominique, Fayoumi, Hamburg, Houdan, Java, La Fleche, Lakenvelder, Marans, Minorca, New Hampshire Red, Old English Game, Orpington, Plymouth Rock, Rosecomb, Sebright, Silkie, Sussex, Naked Neck (also called a Turken), Welsumer, Wyandotte (Avoid all-white individuals; they're more easily spotted by predators than colored and patterned varieties of the same breeds.)

Breeds that tolerate confinement reasonably well
Araucana, Ameraucana, Australorp, Barnvelder, Brahma, Buckeye, Cochin, Cornish, Crevecoeur, Dominique, Dorking, Faverolles, Houdan, Java, Jersey Giant, La Fleche, Lakenvelder, Langshan, Leghorn, Naked Neck (also called a Turken), New Hampsire Red, Orpington, Plymouth Rock, Polish, Rhode Island Red, Silkie, Sultan, Sussex, Welsumer, Wyandotte

Breeds that don't tolerate confinement well
Ancona, Andalusian, Buttercup, Cubalaya, Fayoumi, Hamburg, Malay, Minorca, Modern Game, Old English Game, Spanish White Faced, Sumatra

Think Rare

When choosing a breed of chicken to keep, think rare. Hybrid super-layers and super-broilers are so good at what they do that, for decades, everyday egg and meat chicken raisers bought super chicks, to the detriment of many worthy heritage breeds.

Some breeds are already lost. Others, like these on the American Livestock Breeds Conservancy's watch list, could easily go the way of the dodo, too.

Critical

Fewer than five hundred breeding birds in North America, with five or fewer primary breeding flocks: Andalusian, Aseel, Buckeye*, Buttercup, Campine, Catalina, Chanteclar, Crevecoeur, Delaware*, Dorking, Faverolle, Holland*, Houdan, Java*, La Fleche, Malay, Redcap, Russian Orloff, Spanish, Sumatra

Watch

Fewer than five thousand breeding birds in North America, with ten or fewer primary breeding flocks. Also included are birds which present genetic or numerical concerns or which have a limited geographic distribution: Brahma, Cochin, Cornish (non-industrial), Dominique*, Hamburg, Jersey Giant*, Minorca, New Hampshire*, Polish, Rhode Island White*

Rare

Fewer than one thousand breeding birds in North America, with seven or fewer primary breeding flocks: Ancona, Lakenvelder, Langshan, Sussex

Study

Breeds which are of interest but lack either definition or genetic or historical documentation: Araucana, Cubalaya*, Egyptian Fayoumis, Hungarian Yellow, Iowa Blue*, Lamona*, Modern Game, Nankin, Old English Game, Sebright, Shamo, Sultan

Recovering

Breeds which were once listed in one of the other categories and which have exceeded Watch category numbers but are still in need of monitoring: Australorp, Leghorn (non-industrial), Orpington, Plymouth Rock (non-industrial)*, Rhode Island Red*, Wyandotte*

Visit the ALBC's Watch List at http://www.albc-usa.org/wtchlist.html and follow links to information about most of these breeds. Call (919) 542-5704 or e-mail (albc@albc-usa.org) for the names of breeders in your area.

American Livestock Breeds Conservancy Watch List (as of February 1, 2004)
* North American breeds

The waxy appearance of our barred cochin bantam rooster Dumuzi's comb and wattle is a sign of a healthy chicken. Discolored or swollen areas indicate possible maladies such as influenza or tuber-culosis. Disease can spread through a flock in just a few days.

ther than necessary. Some hatcheries will replace chickens that are dead on arrival, but others won't. Read the guarantee before orderings chicks from a particular place. If the service is available, pay to have your chicks vaccinated for Marek's Disease. This can only be done when they're newly hatched, meaning it's now or never, and it's better to be safe than sad.

Be aware that you can't mail order five or six chicks. For the birds to stay warm enough in transit, a certain number of bodies must be in the shipping box, generating heat. It generally takes about twenty-five large fowl chicks or twenty-five to thirty-five bantams to do the trick. Some hatcheries allow you to order Guinea keets or other similar size hatchlings to fill the quota. You can also find others interested in buying a few chicks and place a co-op order shipped to one address.

If you don't want to deal with roosters, buy sexed pullets. Straight run chicks are cheaper but at least half will be cockerels. If you can raise and butcher the excess roosters, fine. Otherwise, buy just two or three sexed roos to add to the mix—or none at all. Hens don't need roosters to lay eggs.

Before your chicks arrive, assemble everything you'll need to feed, water, and brood them (keeping them warm inside a heated enclosure). Have the brooder box ready and waiting. We'll talk more about this in Chapter 5.

Be home the day your chicks are scheduled to arrive. In most cases, they

The Chicken Carry

When you go someplace to buy full-grown chickens, go prepared! Unless they've been hand tamed, they won't sit quietly in your lap on the way home. Airline-style plastic dog crates make good chicken limousines.

Another option is a sturdy, lidded cardboard box punched with holes. If you do put a chicken in your lap, bring a towel to cover it and wear long sleeves because scared chickens scratch.

Another thing beginners may not know: don't carry chickens by their legs! It can hurt them, it's undignified, and it scares them silly. People think chickens don't mind this position because they don't flop. Well, can you say, "shock?"

You should carry a chicken close to your body with your right arm hugging his body against yours. Then, your right hand can hold his feet while your left hand can support his chest. Give your chickens a break! How would you like to be carried around upside down?

—*Marci Roberts, Springfield, Mo.*

These well-fenced, covered enclosures comfortably house several pens of chickens, geese, and ducks. No matter the size of your coop, invest in proper fencing to keep your flock safe from predators.

won't be delivered to your door; someone from the post office will call you to pick them up. When you arrive for the delivery, open the box of chicks in the presence of a postal worker who will verify your claim should any of them be dead. Then rush your new birds straight home to a cozy brooder box, water, and feed. Don't take side trips with your chicks in tow.

Feed stores frequently offer day-old chicks for sale. Breed selection may be limited (mail order chicks may be your only option if you've decided to buy a rare or unusual breed) and feed store chicks aren't often sexed. However, you can choose the ones you want, buy just a few, and get them home quickly. Select bright-eyed, active chicks with straight shanks, toes, and beaks. Pick them up to see if they have dried drop-

pings stuck to their tiny bottoms; this is called pasting or **pasty butt**. Crusty, dried droppings can block a chick's vent, making it impossible for him to eliminate. You can wash or pick off these droppings, but pasty butt may recur. Don't buy problems—it's best to avoid afflicted chickies.

THE BIG GUYS

If you don't want to deal with tiny chicks and you're lucky, you might be able to buy sixteen- to twenty-two-week-old, almost-ready-to-lay females called **started pullets**. Initially, they cost more per bird, but you won't have the expense of brooding them and feeding them for months, so they can actually be a great buy.

Nowadays, pet shops often carry grown chickens. Pratt's Pet Store, an

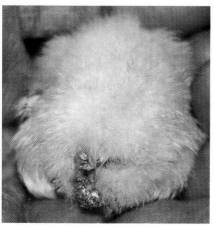

Avoid purchasing chicks such as this one who suffers from pasty butt, a condition where dried droppings prevent him from eliminating. More common among mail order chicks who are packed tightly for safe shipping, pasty butt is best remedied by washing the bird's behind with warm, soapy water.

institution in upscale Glendale, Arizona, sold eight hundred adult hens and more than thirteen thousand baby chicks of more than one hundred breeds in 2002—that's a whole lot of cluckers! Breeders sometimes part with a few hens or breeding trio (a cock and two hens), and you can often find chickens for sale at country flea markets, poultry swap meets, or via classified and bulletin board ads. However, buying adult chickens can be risky. Not all sellers are scrupulously honest and it's easy to buy someone else's problem hens.

Ideally, you should only buy fowl from flocks enrolled in the USDA's National Poultry Improvement Plan (NPIP). These birds are certified free of pullorum and typhoid and healthier than your run-of-the-mill chicken. Barring these issues, choose active, alert, clear-eyed chickens with smooth, glossy feathers and bright, fleshy, waxy combs and wattles. Refuse birds that cough, wheeze, or have discharge or diarrhea. Tip the chicken forward and scope out the area around its vent, and also check under its wings. If you spy insects or eggs and you don't want to deal with parasites, you'd best not buy the bird.

If you want eggs or eating chickens, you must buy young ones. Young adults have smooth shanks, older birds' shanks are dry and scaly and their skin is thick and tough. Cockerels have wee nubs where their spurs will grow and some pullets have them, too; long spurs denote an older bird. Press on the chicken's breastbone; a youngster's is flexible, while old chickens have rigid breastbones.

HOW MANY CHICKENS?

The answer: a resounding "it depends." If you're new at chicken keeping, don't overextend yourself. Start small and learn as you go. The downside to this advice is that introducing new birds to an established flock upsets its pecking order and spawns stress. Overall, it's better for your birds to hatch out a new hierarchy than for you bite off more than you can chew.

By the same token, if you're experienced, or you're certain about how many you want to keep, you'll save your chickens a lot of stressful infighting—and possibly disease—by buying all the birds you need up front, then maintaining a closed flock until you start back at square one again.

Unless you can spend a lot of quality time with a pet chicken (as you might a

These two colorful birds enjoy free run of the farm. Check your city's laws before allowing yours to free range—some ordinances may restrict such practices or even outlaw chicken keeping altogether.

house chicken), buy at least two. Chickens are sociable birds; a solitary cock or hen will be lonely.

You should also buy at least one layer hen per family member, more if your family eats lots of eggs or if you choose a dual-purpose breed. If you plan to maintain a closed flock (and it's wise to do so), you should allow for several years' flock mortality. In order to do this purchase 10-20 percent more baby chicks than you initially think you'll need. Don't buy more birds than you can properly house. We'll talk more about this in Chapter 3.

OUT IN THE FOWL ZONE

Check with your local zoning board before buying chickens. If you live in a strictly rural area, you're probably all right, but if your hobby farm is nestled on the edge of even the smallest municipality, you might not be allowed to keep fowl.

Surprisingly, many of the nation's biggest cities permit the keeping of a few backyard hens, so if you're not living on your dream farm yet, chances are you can still have chickens. Most city ordinances specify how many hens you may have and nearly all prohibit roosters.

Some require you to gain permission from your neighbors (it's a good idea anyway), and they may designate how far your coop must be situated from property lines. Check into local zoning laws before bringing home any birds.

CHAPTER THREE

Chicken Shack or Coop de Ville?

C hickens aren't choosy. Whether simple shack or luxurious villa, as long as the accommodations you provide meet their basic housing needs, your birds will be tickled pink—or feathery—with them. A coop must shelter its inhabitants from wind, rain, snow, and sun and protect them from chicken-swiping varmints. It also needs to be reasonably well lit and ventilated and roomy enough for the number of birds it houses (crowding causes scores of problems). When your chickens go inside, they should find sanitary bedding, roosts, nesting boxes, feeders, and waterers. For your flock's continuing comfort and for your sake, the coop should be easy to access and clean as well.

The specific type of structure you need depends on many factors. Of first consideration are the breed and type of your chickens. For example, when it comes to indoor living space, laying hens, who will be around for many years, demand more space than broiler chickens, who have much shorter life expectancies. Bantams require less indoor space than ten-pound Jersey Giants. Outdoors, a 3-foot uncovered enclosure will keep Jerseys safely contained, but will never do for flying bantams. If you don't provide the latter with a tall, covered run, you may find your entire flock going over the wall.

Climates and landscapes also shape your housing decisions. In northern climes, for instance, chicken abodes must be insulated to spare your birds frostbitten wattles, combs, and toes. In torrid southern locales, how to afford relief from the heat will be a major concern.

The cost of materials, time, and aesthetics should be factored in as well. For example, chicken keepers without a lot of spare cash might decide to build a coop themselves rather than hiring a carpenter or buying a prefab unit. Of course, they will have to live with the results. While almost anyone can construct a functional coop from scratch, using scrounged materials at very little cost, the finished product may not jibe with a builder's preconceived image of the perfect poultry chateau. By contrast, other keepers may have the requisite carpentry skills, but not the time, to create their own chicken villas.

No matter how excited you are to get started, don't pick up that hammer—or let anyone else pick it up—until you've made sure the site is right. The where of coop building is as important as the form and method of it. You don't want to have to raze a half-constructed henhouse after a visitor helpfully points that it's too close to the neighbor's fence.

Many hobby farms are located in the suburbs, which means their coops are subject to municipal codes.

Not the least among the factors to consider when determining how and where to house your new flock are your own wishes. Remember why you decided to keep chickens in the first place. If watching hens peck in the yard will soothe your soul, it makes little sense to shut them away where you can't see them. If, however, chicken poop on your saddles makes your toes curl, locking young broilers in a chicken yard so they don't invade your tack stall is a better option.

YOUR COOP: BASIC REQUIREMENTS

Access, lighting, ventilation, insulation, and flooring all need to be carefully considered as you plan your coop. Think in terms of easy access for you and your flock—but *not* for predators. You'll need to determine how to provide the right amount of lighting and ventilation without compromising the effectiveness of

A homemade structure makes a fine grower coop for this flock of light Brahma pullets and cockerels. Vic Griggs of Thayer, Missouri, crafted this inexpensive enclosure using a secondhand truck topper and standard chicken wire.

This building originally designed to house emus at the Griggs' farm now serves as a chicken coop. When hawks keep their distance, the chickens enjoy the run of a chain-link fenced yard. When danger threatens, a covered rear pen shields them from predation.

your insulation. Knowing which flooring material to use and which to avoid will save you from a lot of future aggravation.

ACCESS

Your coop will need at least two doors: one for you and one or more for your birds. If your coop is low and close to the ground (a good design in northern climes, where body heat is wasted in taller structures), your door might simply be a hinged roof. With this kind of simple opening, you can easily feed and water your birds, tidy the coop, and gather eggs. If the coop is a standard, upright model, it should swing inward so chickens are less likely to escape when you open the door. Chicken doors (14 inches tall by 12 inches wide) can be cut in outer walls about 4-8 inches from the ground. Use the cutout to fashion a ramp. Affix full-width molding (for traction) every 6 inches along its inside surface, then hinge it at the bottom so the door swings out and down. Fit it with a secure latch so you can bar the door at night. If raccoons are a problem in the area, choose a fairly complex latch; if a toddler can open the lock, then a raccoon can unlock it easily.

LIGHTING AND VENTILATION

Light is essential to chickens' health and happiness; natural lighting is better than bulbs and lamps. If you want your hens to lay year-round, you must wire your coop and install fixtures. Sliding windows work best; chickens can't roost on them when they're open. Every window must be tightly screened, even if your chickens can't fly. If predators can wriggle their way around or through those screens, they will. Don't use 1-inch chicken wire or poultry netting; you'll need ½- to ¾-inch galvanized mesh to keep wee beasties such as weasels and mink at bay. If you live in frigid winter climes, large south side windows are a must; they admit lots of winter light and radiant heat. In general, allow at least 1 square foot of window for each 10 square feet of floor space. If you live where temperatures rarely dip below freezing, install even more windows. It's hard to let in too much light.

Extra windows also create cooling, healthful cross-ventilation when summer heat is an issue. Install the extra windows on your coop's north wall and possibly east one too. Your coop must be properly ventilated. Chickens exhale up to thirty-five times per minute, releasing vast amounts of heat, moisture, and carbon dioxide into their environment.

Their lungs won't sustain constantly breathing heavy, toxic air, so faulty coop ventilation quickly leads to respiratory distress. Where large windows (and lots of them) aren't possible, saw 6-inch circular or 2-by-6-inch rectangular ventilation openings high along one or more non-windowed walls. Unplug these vents when extra air is needed, and close them tightly when it's frigid outside. Chickens can weather considerable heat or cold when their housing is dry and draft free, but they don't do well in smelly, damp conditions. If your nose smells ammonia as you enter or open your coop, it's not adequately ventilated. Do something immediately to fix this problem.

Floor Space Requirements

The minimum amount of floor space needed per chicken depends on several factors, including bird type, the presence of indoor roosts, and the size of outdoor run.

Free-range chickens and chickens with adequate outdoor runs and indoor roosts:
Heavy breeds—4 sq. ft. per bird
(2 sq. ft., if slaughtered before 16 weeks of age)
Light breeds—3 sq. ft. per bird
Bantams—2 sq. ft. per bird

Confined chickens without access to outdoor runs:
Heavy breeds—10 sq. ft. per bird
(6 sq. ft., if slaughtered before 16 weeks of age)
Light breeds—8 sq. ft. per bird
Bantams—5 sq. ft. per bird

INSULATION

To get your chickens through winters as unforgiving as those in northern Minnesota, the coop must be well insulated. If money is scarce, you can insulate only the coop's north wall and bank outside by using hay or straw bales stacked at least two deep. Another ploy: bank with snow up against the coop; shovel, push, or bucket it as far up the sides as you can. Window height is good, if you can manage. If it's still too cold inside the coop, you'll need a heat lamp. But remember: fallen heat lamps can, and often do, spark fires. So install your heat lamp in a reasonably safe location and use it only when really needed.

Chickens can die in temperatures higher than 95 degrees. If sizzling, muggy summers are common in your locale, make sure your coop and outdoor enclosures are situated in partial shade—or plant vegetation around your chickens' lodgings to partially shade it; giant pumpkin or bottle gourd vines on trellises are helpful. Insulation helps repel daytime heat, and fans generate badly needed airflow. Opt for light-colored or corrugated metal roofing and paint external surfaces a matte white color to reflect the heat. Avoid overcrowding by allowing additional space for each of your birds; overcrowding leads to higher indoor temperatures and humidity.

FLOORING

Your coop's floor may be constructed of concrete, wood, or plain old dirt. Concrete is rodent-proof and easy to clean, but comparatively expensive. Wood must be elevated on piers or blocks; it looks nice but can be hard to clean and periodically needs replacing.

Well-drained dirt floors work fine. However, if a dirt floor is poorly drained or allowed to become mucky, you'll have a sheer disaster on your hands.

Using the best-bet deep bedding system you'll blanket your floor of choice with a cushy layer of absorbent material to keep things tidy and fresh.

Chopped straw (wheat straw is best) or wood shavings are ideal; rice or peanut hulls, sawdust, dry leaves, and shredded paper work well, too. You'll

A rustic A-frame coop on the edge of the garden makes a fine summer home for these pullets working in our chicken tractor.

line the floor 8-10 inches deep. After it's in, you'll continue to remove messes and add more material when necessary.

Once or twice a year, strip everything back to floor level and start again. Deep bedding nicely insulates a chicken coop floor, it's the essence of simplicity, and it works!

Your Coop: Basic Furnishings

Basic coop furnishings include roosts, nest boxes for laying hens, feeders, and watering stations. Roosts are the elevated poles or boards on which chickens prefer to sleep. Roosting helps them feel safer at night, making these perches a must if you want happy hens. Keeping yourself happy makes nesting boxes a necessity—unless you like going on egg hunts or prefer your eggs precracked. Contentment and peace for everyone means making sure that there's more than one set of waterers and feeders and that they're well placed.

Roosts and Nesting Boxes

In the winter, roosted birds fluff their feathers and cover their toes; they tend to stay warmer that way. Roosts can be as simple as old wooden ladders propped against a chicken coop's inner walls. If you use a ladder, tack the top to the wall.

Then, make sure the bottom is out far enough from the wall so birds settled on one rung don't poop on flockmates roosting on rungs below. If you build traditional stair-stepped roosts for your birds, set the bottom perch about 2 feet from the floor and higher rungs an additional foot apart. Two-by-two boards with rounded edges make ideal roosts for full-size chickens; 1-inch rounded boards or 1-inch dowel rods are fine for bantam breeds. Tree branches of the same diameters make fine roost rails too. But don't use plastic or metal perches; chickens require textured perches that their feet

Hens sometimes choose unlikely places to lay eggs such as the straw-filled bucket this girl selected as a nesting spot.

Toyland for Your Chicks

No-nonsense egg and meat producers may scoff, but for the rest of us, chicken toys in the coop are a nice touch. They're optional, but your birds will love such diversions. Happy chickens develop fewer stress-induced vices and they tend to lay a lot more eggs.

Poultry keepers theorize that stressed birds lay fewer eggs and are far more prone to disease and cannibalism than well-cared-for birds.

can easily grip. Allow 10 inches of perch space for each heavyweight chicken in the coop; 8 inches and 6 inches for light breeds and bantams, respectively.

Wherever you place your roosts, make certain sleeping chickens aren't perched in cross-drafts. Check frequently and move them if necessary.

Nesting Boxes

Hens instinctively seek dark, secluded spots to lay their eggs. Unless you provide nesting boxes, free-range hens sneak off to lay in nooks and crannies and you may never find them! Confined hens plop eggs out wherever they can, which can result in poop-splotched, cracked eggs. Specially designed nesting boxes with slanted tops and perches in front work best (you can buy ready-made wooden, metal, or injection-molded plastic ones from poultry supply houses). However, any sturdy cubicle with a top, a bottom, three enclosed sides, and bedding inside will do nicely.

Make sure the box is larger than the chicken and leave the top off in steamy summer climates. A 14-inch wooden cube with one open side makes an ideal nesting box for full-size hens; 12-inch cubes accommodate bantams with ease.

If you use a regular box, attach a 3- to 4-inch lip across the bottom front to keep bedding and eggs from spilling out. Mount the unit 2 feet from the floor in the darkest corner of the coop. Provide one nesting box for every four or five hens.

Feeders and Waterers

Place at least two sets of commercially made feeders and waterers in every coop and locate each set as far from the others as you can. This prevents guarding by militant high-ranking flock members and causing lowest-ranking chickens to starve. Instead of setting units on the floor, install them so the bottoms of the waterers and the top lips of the feeders are level with the smallest birds' backs. They'll stay cleaner that way and your chickens will waste less food. Be sure to provide one standard hanging tube-style feeder per twenty-five chickens. If you prefer trough feeders, take into consideration that there should be 4 inches of dining space per bird when deciding what size to purchase.

Outdoor Runs: Sunshine and Fresh Air

Another way to keep your chickens

The Comforts of Home

Be sure to provide a shade area for your flock in the outdoor run. No trees? Stretch a tarp across one corner on steamy summer days. Hook it to the fence with bungee cords; a woven wire armature underneath will help secure the tarp in place.

Chickens enjoy lounging under outdoor shelters when it rains. So, if you leave the tarp up when it rains, use an ice pick, awl, or large nail to jab a few holes so runoff can drain. Don't poke holes near the center where your birds gather.

While you're at it, add a sand pit for dust bathing as well!

happy and healthy is to get them into sunshine and fresh air almost every day. To do that, you'll probably need a chicken pen (or run) attached to your coop. Chickens can free range—wander wherever they like—but "where they like" may be your garden (or your neighbor's garden!), or in your garage or barn, or in places where stray dogs or wild things can attack. To save their skins and your infinite vexation, consider a fenced-in area.

FENCING THEM IN

Chicken runs are traditionally crafted of chicken wire (also called poultry netting) that is a flimsy, 1-inch mesh woven into a honeycomb pattern. If a dog or larger varmint wants to get at your chickens, this lightweight wire is not going to be a deterrent. If you value your birds, don't use chicken wire except for indoor applications and chicken run ceilings. Workable alternatives include substantial posts with attached medium- to heavy-duty yard fencing or sturdy welded wire sheep panels (sometimes installed two panels high), or electroplastic poultry netting.

If predators, including dogs, are an ongoing headache, a strong electric charger and two strands of electric wire fencing can provide effective but cheap insurance. String one strand on 10-inch extension insulators 4 inches from the ground, along the outside bottom of the run. Using the same type of

This Dominique hen nibbles the grass through her double-fenced enclosure. The coop's outer layer of livestock paneling is more effective at keeping predators out than its flimsier inner layer of standard chicken wire, which is better at keeping chickens in.

Our hen Gracie preferred living in the sheepfold to life among her peers. So we fastened a dog carrier four feet up the wall to create a private nesting box that won't get bumped by the sheep.

insulator, stretch another strand parallel to the fence's top fence. They'll prevent hungry critters from tunneling under your chicken run fence or scaling its perimeters.

Allow at least 10 square feet of fenced run for each heavy chicken in your flock, 8 square feet for light breeds, and 4 square feet for bantams. In general, you can contain your chickens with a fence 4-6 feet high. However, most bantams and certain light full-size breeds can neatly sail over 6-foot barriers. Keep them in by installing netting over the enclosure.

The Location

Don't create your coop area too far from utilities, especially if you must carry water or run a hose or electrical extension cord from your house, garage, or barn. This will simply be a hassle for you if not taken into consideration. Make sure your coop area is reasonably distant from neighbors' property lines, especially when setback regulations are part of municipal or county codes.

Take into consideration the dryness of the ground when selecting a location; choose a well-drained area where storm runoff and melting snow won't make chicken coop floors and outdoor enclosures a continual, sodden mess. Remember, your coop area should be close enough for you to enjoy your chickens since that is why you wanted them in the first place.

Owls and Weasels and 'Possums, Oh My!

It's no fun—for you or your birds—when hungry midnight marauders visit the chicken coop. The best way to thwart potential predators is to lock your birds inside a safe, secure chicken coop at night. Another approach, if it's legal in your state, is to humanely trap and relocate bothersome nighttime marauders.

Measures for Keeping the Varmints Out

After sundown, every door, window, and any other crack or portal in any outside wall should be tightly blocked or screened. To be effective, screening must be small-holed and made of strong material. A mink or weasel can easily slip through 1-inch chicken wire, and larger species can simply rip it down. Choose 3/4-inch or smaller mesh galvanized hardware cloth for screening windows and building outdoor enclosures to save your chickens' lives.

To discourage chicken-swiping predators, install concrete block foundations into coop floors, set at least two rows high. In addition, bury outdoor enclosure fencing at least 8-12 inches into the earth. Make sure the buried fencing is toed outward, away from the fence line. If winged predators, such as daytime hawks or nighttime owls, pursue your birds, cover the outdoor enclosure with chicken wire; for this purpose, it works nicely.

If your birds range free and you live where chicken-thieving hawks wreak havoc, think camouflage. For example, don't choose a white-feathered breed.

Plant ground cover—bushes, hedges, and flowerbeds—so your chickens can hole up in the greenery when predators soar above.

If predators are simply getting into your feed you can *secure* container lids with bungee cords. Do this by securing bungee cords to eyebolts set in the feed room wall. The key word is secure for both your chickens and their feed.

Trapping Intruders

If it's legal in your state, you may decide to take care of the problem of predators by trapping and relocating them. The first step is to figure out what's killing your chickens; this will enable you to bait the live trap with species-specific yummies.

A skunk lived in this hole under our chicken house's foundation.

A carefully concealed Havahart trap helped capture the critter alive so we could relocate him to a distant wildlife preserve.

Determining Who Done It

You can figure out the identity of your midnight raider by discovering what was taken and what was left. Opossums, skunks, and raccoons savor chicken eggs. They may raid your coop without killing a bird. A dead bird, however, doesn't rule them out. They might dine on meat and eggs during the same visit.

When opossums have a hankering for chicken, they'll usually kill a single bird per visit; typically only the abdomen will be eaten. Raccoons visit a coop infrequently, once a week or so. They prefer heads and crops; more than one chicken may be killed. If skunks invade your chicken house, they're also likely chew off one or more chickens' heads; worse, a lingering aroma of eau de phew will generally give them away. A neat stack of dead chickens—with necks eaten and heads missing—suggests the culprits are probably minks or weasels. Foxes usually are blamed for most chicken coop predation, but if you find dead chickens, foxes likely aren't involved.

They carry their prey away with them—as do bobcats, coyotes, and predatory birds—usually without leaving a trace.

If chickens are missing and you suspect foxes, bait live traps with chicken entrails or raw chicken, dead mice, or commercial lures. These work for the wily coyote, too, but you'll need a much

Catching the Smart Ones

Try camouflaging outdoor traps inside and out with fresh or dried grasses. In a coop setting, straw or hay works well. This could help you catch the smart predator.

This daytime enclosure is constructed of lightweight chicken wire; while acceptable in areas with little predation problems, a more secure tactic such as double-fencing is more effective for areas with pesky intruders.

larger trap to catch him. Opossums like fruit, especially melon or apples; raccoons fancy marshmallows, sweet corn, canned creamed corn, and honey.

In general, baits of choice include fresh fish, chicken heads or entrails, fresh raw liver, crisp bacon, fish-flavored moist cat food, and table scraps. Whatever your bait, be sure to replace it every day.

Catching the Suspect

Heavy-gauge wire live traps can be used for humane trapping and relocating. You can purchase them at most hardware stores or order them online. If you don't want to buy, contact your city or county animal control officer or humane society to see if you can get one on loan. Check out rental centers as well; they often carry these traps in stock. If you buy a live trap, read the instructions. If you rent or borrow one, ask an experienced live trapper to teach you how to operate it efficiently and humanely.

Keep the animal's suffering to a minimum. Check traps at least three times a day (more frequently is better). When trapping during the day, make certain the traps are set in the shade. If you find an animal in the trap, immediately shroud the entire enclosure in a sheet or towel to calm the inhabitant. Promptly take him to your local animal control officer or relocate him at least five miles from your property in an uninhabited area that offers an abundance of species-specific natural food, water, and shelter.

If you catch more than one of a kind, release them in the same location. Wear gloves when transporting trapped animals; frightened wild things bite hard!

One more word of advice: you can easily live trap and release skunks, but it takes special finesse not to get sprayed. Know what you're doing before you try.

BUILDING A CHEAPER CHICKEN COOP

If your desire to keep chickens exceeds your ability to buy or build a standard chicken coop, don't worry: chickens can adapt to simple accommodations. If you keep them dry, safe, and out of drafts, they'll be happy. Consider the following inexpensive options.

You can build chicken accommodations into existing structures such as your garage or back porch, the kids' abandoned playhouse, and unused sheds and storage buildings. Build coop-style quarters or house your chickens in cages. Show chicken fanciers often cage their birds in wire rabbit-style hutches. Buy them new, or from a rabbitry that is going out of business, or build them yourself.

It's best to forgo keeping heavy breed chickens if they must live in cages; continually standing on wire floors will likely damage their feet. Allow 7 square feet of cage floor space for light breed chickens or 6 square feet for bantams. Place a 2-foot-by-2-foot sheet of salvaged cardboard box stock in one corner where inhabitants can rest their feet; replace it with a new piece when it gets soiled.

Caged chickens appreciate roosts—affix them at least 6 inches from the floor—and boredom-squelching amusements such as toys.

Keep a pet chicken or two in a dog crate or a solid-bottomed rabbit cage in

This solid-bottomed rabbit cage serves as an inexpensive coop that can be brought indoors. Avoid models with wire floors or install cardboard or wood over the flooring—heavy breed chickens are especially susceptible to foot injuries from long days on wire–bottom cages.

Joys and Toys

• Consider diversions for the flock. Movable outside coops (chicken tractors) make happy, healthy birds. Inside toys and diversions are important. Our chickens play tether lettuce (mesh bags with greens suspended from the ceiling.) Toys for caged birds are enjoyed for a while. Mirrors and bells are a hit. Rotate the toys.

• Our flock likes to peck at treats placed on empty large margarine tubs. It sounds like rain on a tin roof when they pick up grain. They like the sound, too.

• We usually have one bird in each hatch named Bucket. They love to peck at the bucket into which we place clumps of manure. (We clean the shavings daily.)

• I've heard that large flexible pipe (drain tile) is a hit if the birds can fit easily inside.

• Chickens in the wild investigate and scratch. Their brains are wired for cautiously (they are a prey species) investigating new situations. Ramps and things to duck under and fit inside are popular.

• There needs to be somewhere for a sad, slightly sick, or not aggressive bird to sit and read a book. They need an escape route.

• Chickens love to scratch. A sand box with a little grain will give a thrill.

• They love greens. A box framed with two-by-fours with a wire mesh on top will let you grow grass but keep them above the grass so they don't destroy it; they can only get the long pieces.

• Perching birds (some Silkies too) love varied heights not just the same old perch.

—Alan Stanford, Whitewater, Wisc.

Chicken A-Cord

Build your chicken house within two long heavy-duty extension cords' reach from your house or garage. Then you can have electricity when you want it and it's less costly than hiring an electrician.

—Mandy Anderson, Anoka, Minn.

The Chicken Golden Rule

The Chicken Golden Rule: If it's possible for a chicken to hurt itself on something, it will find a way. This is important to remember when building a coop because if you leave that one little piece of sharp wire poking out, somehow, some bird will find a way to impale itself on it no matter how remote the chance may seem. People should get down on their hands and knees—at chicken level—and really LOOK at their finished coop to try and spot chicken hazards, just like new parents do for babies around the house—after all, having birds is like having an eternal two-year-old.

—Susan Mennealy, Norwalk, Calif.

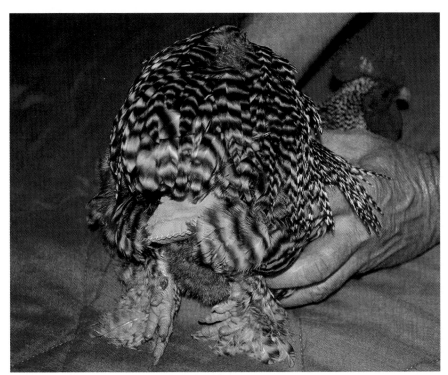

Washable chicken diapers are a solution to a messy problem with chickens that roam the home. This cochin bird's fluffy feathers conceal the stretchy harness that holds the diaper in place.

your home. Many folks do. Change their litter often and fit them with washable fabric chicken diapers when they roam the house. As one owner of an indoor chicken succinctly says, "What's the difference between a chicken and a parrot except $3,000?" Makes sense to me!

A large wooden packing crate fitted with a hinged roof makes a dandy indoor or outdoor coop. Prop the lid open during the day (if you keep flying breeds you'll have to fashion a screen) and close it at night. Outdoors, install a latchable dog door in one side and attach a small fenced run.

If appearance doesn't matter, fashion a funky, cost-effective walk-in coop out of tarps, a welded wire cattle panel (or two), and scrap lumber. Coops of standard designs can be crafted using secondhand lumber and other scrounged or recycled goodies. It's amazing what can be done with plastic tarps if aesthetics don't count.

Nappies for Indoors

Chicken diapers aren't what you think. They're neat, stretchy pouches covering just the bare essentials— cage bird fanciers use smaller versions on their parrots and cockatoos.

After a few trial runs, most birds forget they're wearing them. They make having birds (especially big ones, like chickens) in the house a lot more fun.

CHAPTER FOUR

Chow for Your Hobby Farm Fowl

While your chickens' nutritional needs vary depending on age, sex, breed, and use, their diets must always include water, protein, vitamins, minerals, carbohydrates, and fats in adequate quantities and proper balance. All chicken keepers are in agreement on this point. But when it comes to the question of how best to supply all those dietary elements, it's a different story. Ask any group of fanciers how each feeds his or her chickens and you'll find two distinct camps—those who never feed their birds anything except commercial mixes, and those who never feed their birds commercial mixes without supplementing them. Opinion runs high on both sides about which approach is better.

Which one you should take really depends on your primary reason for keeping chickens. If you raise birds strictly for their meat or eggs, commercial feed is the way to go. Commercial bagged rations are formulated to serve up optimal nutrition, thus creating optimal production. Supplementing commercial feed with treats, table scraps, scratch (a whole or cracked grain mixture chickens adore), or anything else will upset that delicate nutritional balance.

However, if like us you see your chickens as friends and don't care if their growth is slightly slower if they produce fewer eggs, then consider supplementing their diets. They'll appreciate the variety, and you'll appreciate the much lower cost of a supplemented diet.

WATER

Consider this: an egg is roughly 65 percent water, a chick 79 percent, a mature chicken 55 to 75 percent. Blood is 90 percent water. Chickens guzzle two to three times as much water as they eat in food, depending on their size, type (layers require more water than broiler chickens), and the season—up to two or three cups per day. So whether you use a commercial or home-based diet, your chickens require free access to fresh, clean water.

Chickens need water to soften what they eat and carry it through their digestive tracts; many of the digestive and nutrient absorption processes depend on water. In addition, water cools birds internally during the hot summer months. If you eliminate water from your chickens' diet expect problems immediately. Even a few hours of water deprivation affects egg production.

Chickens don't drink a lot, at any single time, but they drink often. However, water temperature can affect how much they will drink. They don't like to drink hot or icy water, so keep waterers away from heat sources and out of the blazing sun. When temperatures soar, plop a handful of ice cubes in the reservoir every few hours. In the winter, replace regular waterers with heated ones or add a bucket-style immersion heater to a standard metal version. You can also swap iced-up

A large, hanging style waterer, such as this one we use in our daytime enclosure, helps keep your birds' water free of debris.

waterers for fresh ones containing tepid water every few hours. In subzero climates, heated waterers are a must; even a heated dog watering dish is acceptable.

Because chickens are inherently messy, chicken-specific waterers are better than buckets and dishes. Hanging (tube style) models are good; automatic waterers work best of all; and metal waters last longer than plastic ones. Read the instructions that come with the waterer you choose to determine how many units you'll need. Even if one waterer is enough, choose two.

Otherwise bossy, high-ranking chickens in your flock's hierarchy may shoo underlings away from the fountain. (This recommendation goes for feed troughs, too).

Waste Less

Chickens waste about 30 percent of feed in a trough feeder that's full. If the same trough is only half full, however, they waste only 3 percent.

Save yourself time and money by spreading less feed for your chickens in more troughs.

Although hanging waterers can be placed on the floor, hanging them from hooks or rafters with the drinking surface level with your smallest chickens' backs will give the best results. If you can't hang a waterer, make certain it's level, or it will leak.

Whichever type of waterer you use and wherever you hang your waterers, clean and rinse them every day. Scour them once a week (more often in the summer, when they tend to get scummy) using a stiff brush and a solution of about nine parts water to one part chlorine bleach.

COMMERCIAL FEEDS

Whether you buy or mix it yourself, a healthy, happy chicken's diet should provide the following:

- Sufficient protein based on the age and needs of the bird.
- Carbohydrates, a major energy source.
- Thirteen vitamins to support growth, reproduction, and body maintenance—fat-soluble vitamins A, D_3, E, K, and water-soluble vitamins B_{12}, thiamin, riboflavin, nicotinic acid, folic acid, biotin, pantothenic acid, pyridoxine, and choline.
- Macro minerals (those needed in larger quantities) and trace or micro minerals (needed only in minute amounts) to build strong bones and healthy blood cells, supporting enzyme activation and muscle function, and regulating metabolism. Hens require additional minerals, especially calcium, to lay eggs with nice, thick shells.
- Fats for energy and proper absorption of fat-soluble vitamins and as sources of fatty acids, necessary for supporting fertility and egg hatchability.
- Commercial feeds, presented at recommended levels, are designed to meet those needs precisely. To meet protein requirements, commercial feeds include

Most feed stores carry a variety of bagged chicken feeds like these. Be sure to carefully read the sacks' labels. Feed types designed for specific groups of birds may contain ingredients that your birds don't need.

Chicken Feed

Which Commercial Chicken Feed Should You Buy?

Feed Type	Protein Content	Use it	Feed it
Starter (for layers)	18%–20%	As a high-protein feed for fast-growing future laying hens	Until 6 weeks of age
Starter (for broilers)	20%–22%	As an even higher-protein feed for even faster-growing meat chicks of both sexes	Until 6 weeks of age
Grower (for layers)	15%–16%	As a lower-protein feed for pullets	6–20 weeks or until laying begins, whichever comes first
Layer	16%–18% (with additional calcium added)	As a maintenance diet for hens laying eggs for consumption	20 weeks on
Breeder	18% (additional calcium and extra vitamins added	As a maintenance diet for hens laying hatching eggs	As long as hens are used for producing hatching eggs
Finisher (for broilers)	18%–20%	As a lower-protein-than-broiler-starter diet to carry broilers until slaughter	4–6 weeks until slaughter

a variety of high-protein meals made of corn gluten, soybeans, cottonseed, meat, bone, fish, and dried whey. Too much protein can be as bad as too little, so balancing this nutrient is especially tricky.

• Carbohydrates are much easier; they naturally compose a large portion of every grain-based diet. While some of the thirteen vitamins listed above are plentiful in natural foodstuff, commercial feeds cover all bases by adding a vitamin premix. Ground oyster shells or limestone, salt, and trace mineral premix are commercial feed additives designed to meet a chicken's macro and micro mineral needs. As for fats, commercial feeds contain processed meat and poultry fats in measured amounts. Fats provide twice as much energy as other feed ingredients, making them especially useful in starter feeds and growing rations.

• Mixing your own commercial-style feed is an option (and often a must for producers of organic meat or eggs), but it's a complex and nutritionally risky one. Using the commercial feed on the market is convenient and easy.

COMMON INGREDIENTS AND ADDITIVES

Common ingredients in commercial feeds include corn, oats, wheat, barley, sorghum, milo, soybean, and other oilseed meals, cottonseed or alfalfa meal,

Protein

To Create a 15% Protein Layer Ration...

...using a 10% protein (typical) scratch mix of these proportions...	...requires mash containing this amount of protein
half scratch/half mash	20%
two-thirds scratch/one-third mash	25%
three-quarters scratch/one-quarter mash	30%

wheat or rice bran, and meat by-products, such as bonemeal and fishmeal. Ingredients are finely ground to produce easier-to-digest mash; sometimes, they are pelleted or processed into crumbles so there is less wasted food.

Commercial baby chick food is usually medicated; some feeds for older chickens are medicated, too. Each type, designed for a specific group of birds, contains nutrients in slightly different measures, so when buying feed, read the tags and labels to make certain you're buying what your chickens require.

Commercial feeds also contain ingredients that many fanciers don't approve of, such as antibiotics and coccidiostats for birds that don't need them, pellet binders to improve the texture of pelleted feed, and chemical antioxidants to prevent fatty ingredients spoilage. If you'd like to offer your chickens commercial feed but want to avoid the questionable additives, ask your county agricultural agent or feed store representative what "natural" commercial feeds are available locally. Some—such as Purina's SunFresh Start & Grow, Layena, Flock Raiser, and Scratch Grains—can be purchased or ordered in most locales. The Murray McMurray Hatchery sells organic feed, priced to ship post paid to any location in the continental United States. Always be sure to read labels of unfamiliar commercial feed before dishing out the grub. Know what's in there and precisely what amounts to feed.

When feeding commercial products, choose the correct feed: starter, grower, layer, breeder, or finisher. That information will be printed on the label or tag, so always check to be certain.

Don't indiscriminately substitute types. In a pinch, you can adjust a feed's protein level by diluting it with scratch or adding a separate protein supplement, but if the feed mill doesn't offer what you need, it's best to shop elsewhere. Make sure to buy quality feed from a reputable source. If in doubt, major companies such as Purina and Nutrena are reliable bets.

MAINTAINING NUTRITIONAL VALUE AND FRESHNESS

To retain full nutritional value and assure freshness, purchase no more than a two-to four-week supply of commercial feed.

Don't dump new product on top of remaining feed; use up the old feed first or scoop it out and place it on top of the new supply. When storing feed, place it in tightly closed containers and store in a cool, dry place out of the sun. Plastic containers work best, but if plastic-gnawing rodents are a headache, store grain in lidded metal cans. A 10-gallon garbage can—plastic or metal—can hold 50 pounds of feed and makes a neat, ready-made feed bin.

If your chickens refuse the commercial feed, examine it closely. Sniff. It may be musty or otherwise spoiled. If it seems all right, you're probably dealing with picky chickens who prefer scratch, treats, and table scraps. You should cut back on goodies until they eat the chicken ration, too. Distributing treats only in the late afternoon, after they've dined on their regular rations will encourage them to be less picky.

THE SUPPLEMENT APPROACH

According to proponents of supplements, hens fed strictly with commercial feed lay tasteless, thin-shelled supermarket-quality eggs and broilers fed the same diet will taste like packaged store-bought chickens. A push? Maybe. That's something you'll have to decide for yourself. What we present here are methods chicken keepers can use to supplement the diets of their flocks.

GRIT AND OYSTER SHELLS

Since chickens don't have teeth, they swallow grit—tiny pebbles and other hard objects—to grind their food. If your chickens free range or you use easily digestible commercial feed, you won't need to provide your birds with grit.

Otherwise, commercial grit (ground limestone, granite, or marble) can be mixed with their scratch or container-fed to chickens on a free-choice basis.

Ground oyster shell is too soft to function as grit, but it's a terrific calcium booster for laying hens. Feeding oyster shell to hens on a free-choice basis allows the hens to eat it when they wish.

SCRATCH

While university resources advise a straight commercial diet, most hobbyists and small flock owners supplement this with scratch. Scratch is a mixture of two or more whole or coarsely cracked grains, such as corn, oats, wheat, milo, millet, rice, barley, and buckwheat.

Chickens adore scratch grains. Chickens instinctively scratch the earth with their sharp toenails to rake up bugs, pebbles for grit, seeds, and other natural yummies; strewn on their indoor litter or anyplace outdoors, scratch satisfies that urge. Or you can place feed in separate indoor feeders. To preserve its nutritional balance, commercial feed should be supplemented with scratch in measured proportions.

GREENS AND INSECTS

Hobby farmers and poultry enthusiasts often grow "chicken gardens" of cut-and-come-again edibles like lettuce, kale, turnip greens, and chard. Chickens of all types and sizes relish greens. Greens-chomping hens lay eggs with dark, rich yolks.

Insects add protein to chickens' diets. Free-range chickens harvest their own bugs but coop and run-caged birds don't have that chance. Capture katydids, grasshoppers, and other tasty insects to toss to your chickens. If you do, they'll soon come running when they spot you.

GOOD HOME COOKIN'

Chickens happily devour table scraps. Avoid fatty, greasy, salty stuff, anything spoiled, avocados, and uncooked potato peels. Also, strongly scented or flavored scraps, such as onions, garlic, salami, and fish can flavor hens' eggs. Most everything else from your table will work as well, even baked goods, meat, and dairy products. Your chickens will love it.

Many fanciers scramble or fry eggs and feed them back to their chickens.

Egg yolk is a chicken's first food; it's a fine supplement for adult birds of all ages and an ideal use for eggs with cracked or soiled shells. However, if you overfeed your chickens on scratch, greens, veggies, and "people food," some will turn up their beaks when served commercial rations. Unless you devise a balanced diet based on home-mixed victuals, consider them supplements, not first-line chicken feed.

Many folks assume free-range chickens will grow healthy eating seeds, weeds, and bugs. They won't. However, if you supplement free-range findings with scratch or commercial

Two of our farm favorites, Dumuzi and Marge, nosh on lettuce straight from the garden. Veggies are one of many treats chickens appreciate straight from your table.

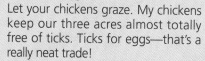

Food Is Not Boring Here!

My chickens get yummy breakfasts every other day (they have leftovers the other days). Oatmeal, rabbit feed (for a nice greens-based meal), raisins, scrambled eggs, cat food (protein—and they love it), apples, leftovers, mac 'n' cheese (a favorite!), green beans, and Cheerios (another favorite).

—*Jennifer Kroll White Lake, Mich., Fluff 'N Strut Silkies, owner*

Chicken Feed Is a Personal Choice

The commercial feeds and university Web sites are geared for highest production per pound of feed, so naturally they're going to advise you to feed only a commercial-formulated diet. It's so easy to control exactly which nutrients go into the chickens using a commercial diet. However, if you watch chickens free range, they eat everything that can't outrun them.

—*Barb Silcott, Milan, Ind.*

Avian Tick Brigade

Let your chickens graze. My chickens keep our three acres almost totally free of ticks. Ticks for eggs—that's a really neat trade!

—*Sharon Jones, Pine City, Minn.*

Oats and Protein

In the summer, instead of feeding regular scratch, give your laying hens whole, plump oats. They like oats, they stay cooler, and they lay more eggs. Also, when my chickens need extra protein, like when they're molting or growing fast, I toss them a handful of dry cat food or meat-based dog kibble twice a day. They gobble it up and it adds lots of protein at a very low price.

—*Marci Roberts, Springfield, Mo.*

feed, your chickens will cheerfully rid your yard and orchard of termites, ticks, Japanese beetles, grasshoppers, grubs, slugs, and dropped fruit. One caveat: they'll also strip your garden clean; think "fenced garden" if you raise free-range chickens.

Chicken Tractors, Pastured Poultry, and Free-Range Chickens... What Does It All Mean?

Most range (also called short-pasture) poultry systems fall into one of three basic categories: free range, pastured poultry, and chicken tractors. The first two systems are used for raising commercial flocks and probably won't interest most who read this book, but they work nicely for hobby farmers seeking ways to raise and market homegrown, value-added products such as natural or organic meat chickens and organic eggs. Chicken tractors are lightweight, bottomless shelter pens designed to move wherever grass control and soil fertility are required. They appeal to small-scale raisers like you and me: maintaining a chicken tractor in your garden not only enriches your soil, it's the perfect way to supplement your birds' diet with yummy greenery, crunchy bugs, worms, and grubs.

In the grand scheme of things, free-range chickens are any that are allowed to roam fenceless and free during the day, returning at night to a coop or shelter in a barn, tree, or where ever else they can find. Free-range chickens, when spoken of in conjunction with today's range poultry management phenomenon, are something else indeed.

They are raised in 8-by-18-foot skid houses set in roomy, clipped grass pastures, which are surrounded by predator-resistant perimeter fencing. Each shelter has a roof, a sturdy floor, and wood-framed 1-inch chicken wire sides.

A mother hen and her little ones enjoy roaming the farm. Today's free-range chickens are commonly protected by predator proof fencing, though the term suggests they have full run of your farm.

They're fitted with roosts, nest boxes (for layers), bulk feeders, and float-valve waterers. Chickens, stocked at the rate of four hundred per acre, are allowed to free range during the day and are confined to their skid houses at night. Spacing can be no less than 150 feet between skid houses or from a skid house to the nearest fence. When grazing around the skid houses grows thin (generally every few months), the skids—chickens and all—are towed to a new location within the pasture. The free-range system is widely used throughout Europe for producing natural and organic meat chickens or eggs; it's the coming thing in North America, too.

Pastured Poultry are raised in 8-by-10-foot portable pens with roofs but no floors and are confined day and night. Each pen contains about eighty chickens. Roosts and nest boxes are provided; feed and water are carried to the chickens. Structures are moved to fresh pasture (with the birds inside of them) once or twice every day.

Chicken tractors are engineered to move around your farm, usually by hand, to areas in need of enrichment. Size depends on the strength of the operator and ranges from 3 by 5 by 2 feet for three or four chickens to a whopping 8 by 12 by 3 feet. Sides are crafted of wood-framed wire mesh; a hinged roof protects inhabitants from

A moveable chicken tractor allows the hobby farmer to designate an area of the land where these chickens help cultivate the garden.

the elements and allows easy operator entry. If you build compact tractors to fit the width of spaces between your garden rows, the chickens will neatly weed and fertilize your garden without tanking up on produce while they do it (water and feed are provided inside the tractor; you'll need to advance the unit once or twice a day). Larger chicken tractors can be set atop spots needing more thorough cultivation over longer periods of time. Chickens are day laborers; they're removed from the tractor at night. It's a great way to cultivate and nourish garden soil while entertaining your chickens. There's a place for a chicken tractor (or two) on most every hobby farm!

These birds, enjoy free ranging in their yard. They return to the safety of a predator-proof enclosure when the sun sets.

CHAPTER FIVE

Chicks, With or Without a Hen

There are few things more enchanting than a clutch of baby chicks. Chances are you'll want to grow some. There are three basic ways to start your chick collection. You can take the quickest and easiest route by buying "ready-made" chicks from a hatchery. If, however, you want to be involved from egg to newborn chick, you can choose the most labor-intensive route instead—incubation. Or you may decide in favor of the old-fashion approach to chick making—with a hen.

Whether you start with hatchery chicks or incubate your own (in an incubator or under a hen), you'll arrive at the same point: with a clutch of chicks to brood.

HATCHERY CHICKS

Most folks begin with hatchery chicks. They're inexpensive, readily available, and if you shop around, you'll find scores of breeds and varieties to choose from. Revisit Chapter Two for a list of mail-order hatcheries and buying tips; reputable mail-order hatcheries are good sources for healthy chicks of the scarcer breeds.

Don't assume you'll have to settle for Leghorns or Cornish Cross chicks when you shop close to home. Phone feed stores in your locale, especially prior to "chick time" (early spring) and ask what they'll be selling this year. Our small-town feed store, Hirsch's in Thayer, Missouri, sells all the standard varieties, but it offers exciting rare breed chickies, too: German Spitzhaubens, Naked Necks, Black Sumatras, Dominiques and Jersey Giants, even Red Jungle Fowl!

The difference between mail-order and local pick-up hatchery chicks is that the former are more likely to be stressed. However, handled correctly on arrival, healthy chicks from solid hatcheries rebound quickly. Most mail-order hatcheries tuck in an extra chick or two for each twenty-five you've ordered, to cover your losses in case a few don't make it.

INCUBATOR CHICKS

If you have access to fertile eggs and a sense of adventure, you can incubate your own chicks. You'll need an incubator and its accessories (a quality thermometer, a hygrometer to measure humidity, and a water pan if the incubator you choose doesn't have a built-in water reservoir). You'll need to build or buy an egg candling unit, too.

Good home incubators are expensive and incubating chicks is exacting work. If the atmospheric conditions

The Griggs family uses this circulating air cabinet incubator for chicken, guinea fowl, duck, and goose eggs.

inside the incubator are off for even a few hours, your eggs very likely won't hatch. Factoring in equipment costs, you can buy a lot of chicks for what it will cost you to hatch them at home.

However, when eggs in your batch begin pipping (when the peeping chickies peck holes in their shells)—what a priceless thrill! So if you want to try home incubation, here are the bare bones basics.

CHOOSING AND MAINTAINING YOUR INCUBATOR

There are two types of incubators: forced air and still air. A forced air incubator is fitted with one or more powerful internal fans that continually circulate air around the eggs. The ones used by hatcheries and commercial growers are monstrous things capable of incubating thousands of eggs set in stacked trays.

Tabletop models designed for hobbyists and small-flock poultry keepers hold from forty to one hundred eggs in a single tray and cost in the neighborhood of $75 to $575. Most are auto-turning units, meaning they turn the eggs for you at predetermined intervals. More expensive models come complete with one or more thermometers and sometimes a hygrometer.

It's easier to maintain constant heat and humidity levels—essential for good hatches—in forced air units.

Temperatures are the same anywhere in a forced air incubator; in still air models, temperatures stratify, so it's considerably warmer near the incubator's lid than it is on

The Griggs family uses this circulating air cabinet incubator for chicken, guinea fowl, duck, and goose eggs. Water pans inside the unit provide humidity essential for a proper hatch. However, not every egg hatches successfully. Bottom right, a chick pipped from this egg, but he couldn't break free of the shell's tough inner membrane.

its egg rack or floor. Forced air incubators are initially more expensive than comparable still units, but they're worth it.

A still air incubator relies on vents set into its sides, top, and bottom for ventilation, which is not a particularly reliable system. Because ventilation is limited, it's more difficult to regulate heat and humidity in still air incubators.

They cost from $12 to $16 for a tiny two-egg model (more toy than incubator, although with careful monitoring, it will certainly hatch eggs) to $85 for a top-of-the-line unit. A few still air models can be retrofitted with forced air fans. It doesn't cost a fortune to get started with these units and, with care, they'll hatch a lot of eggs. However, it's very easy to overheat eggs and essentially cook them. It's a great deal harder to regulate

heat and humidity in a still air incubator.

Both types incorporate see-through lids or transparent observation ports, heating elements, built-in water receptacles or space to set a water pan, and egg racks. Automatic egg turners (which are very nice to have) are optional equipment on all but the most expensive models. Whichever you choose, don't toss the owner's manual! Each brand and model differs from the rest and unless you follow the instructions in the manual provided with your incubator, you're unlikely to have much of a hatch.

It's important to set up the incubator indoors, in a draft free area, out of direct sunlight, and away from heat vents and window air conditioners. It must be thoroughly cleaned and disinfected before and after every hatch.

Two days before setting your fertile eggs, disassemble, scrub, and disinfect your incubator and accessories, then put it back together and fire it up. This gives it a chance to come up to heat and also gives you time to adjust the temperature and humidity.

Temperature, humidity, and ventilation must all be set properly and monitored to ensure successful development of the embryos.

Temperature

Place a trustworthy thermometer in the incubator at egg height. It should not be too close to the heating element and about 1 inch from the floor. In some units, the egg tray itself will do. Some folks play safe and set thermometers in two different locations.

If your incubator has a thermostat, set it at 99-100 degrees for forced air units and 101-102 degrees for those with-out a fan. Inexpensive incubators usually lack thermostats; in that case, follow the owner's manual exactly—you must be able to reliably regulate the heat. A tip: if your incubator is heated with standard light bulbs, use bulbs of different wattages to adjust the heat; a 40-watt bulb is a good one to start with.

Don't add eggs until you've maintained the correct heat and humidity for at least eight hours. The acceptable range is from 97-103 degrees, but the closer you come to the exact degree, the better the hatch. Overheating is worse than the opposite; it's terribly easy to cook those eggs! Check often, at least twice a day. You'll find that your vigilance will pay off in chicks.

Humidity

To prevent moisture loss from your eggs—and to get them to hatch properly—you must control humidity scrupulously. Relative interior humidity

This basic still air incubator contains a batch of chicken, Guinea keet, and wild turkey eggs.

This still air incubator's windows allow observers to keep track of the action inside. The central switch adjusts the unit's temperature.

should run 55-60 percent from days one through eighteen. For the last three days of incubation, humidity should be increased to 65-70 percent. Without a boost of additional moisture pipping chicks stick to their shells. Maintaining that higher humidity level is so vitally important that you must not open your incubator during the final three days of hatching, even to turn the eggs.

You'll need a hygrometer (also called a wet bulb thermometer) to measure the incubator's evaporative cooling effect. Buy one when you order your incubator or from poultry suppliers who sell incubators; a good one costs between $20 and $45. Some resources recommend wrapping cotton around the bulb of a regular thermometer to fashion a homemade version but it's "pound foolish" to improvise. Install the hygrometer so its wick (not its bulb) is sus-

pended in water. To determine relative humidity, compare incubator thermometer temperature and hygrometer (wet bulb thermometer) readings.

The greater the spread, the more evaporation is taking place. Ideally, hygrometer readings will run between eighty-three and eighty-seven. Raise the unit's relative humidity, especially just prior to the three-day hatching period, by increasing the evaporative water surface. Replace your existing water pan with a larger one, add a second pan, or prop one end of a soaked sponge in the existing water pan. You can also use an atomizer to spritz moisture through your incubator's vents.

Ventilation

Oxygen reaches developing chick embryos via the fifteen thousand or so pores in the average eggshell; carbon dioxide exits the same way. Hatching

Humidity

Relative Humidity Calculator

Wet Bulb Reading						Incubator Temperature
97.7	89.0	87.3	85.3	83.3	81.3	100 °F
91.0	90.0	88.2	86.2	84.2	82.2	101 °F
92.7	91.0	89.0	87.0	85.0	83.0	102 °F
70%	65%	60%	55%	50%	45%	**Percent Relative Humidity**

eggs must breathe, or the chicks inside will die. As embryos mature, they require more fresh air. Incubator vents provide ventilation in various ways; read your unit's owner's manual to learn if, when, and how you should adjust the vents.

MANIPULATING THE EGGS

A setting hen rolls her eggs—unintentionally while shifting her weight or intentionally with her beak—several dozen times a day. If she didn't do this, the embryos would stick to their shell membranes and die. With no hen in sight, it's up to you to do the egg turning (as the process is called) necessary for your incubator embryos to thrive.

It's also up to you to check that those embryos are indeed thriving by candling the eggs. Candling eggs is the process of holding an unhatched, incubating egg up to a strong light source to examine the contents inside and determine whether the egg is fertile. Infertile eggs and those that have quit growing need to be removed from the incubator before they begin to rot.

Egg Turning

Turn the eggs first thing in the morning, last thing at night, and at least once during the day; turning them more often is definitely better. Alternate the turns so the side that is down one night will be on top the following night. Use a soft lead pencil to mark one side of each egg with an "x" and the other with an "o" so you can keep track of the turning cycles.

When placing eggs in still air incubators, position them on their sides with their small ends tipped slightly downward; rotate them one-half turn at least three times a day. In forced air incubators, place them small end down and tilted in one direction; tilt them the opposite direction to turn them.

Do not turn eggs during the last three days before hatching. Chicks will be maneuvering into pipping position and moving disorients them. Besides, to maintain constant 65-75 percent relative humidity throughout the pre-hatch period, you don't want to open the incubator for any reason.

Some incubators incorporate automatic egg turners and many that don't

lights, switch your candler on, then one by one, hold the eggs in front of the intense light.

Infertile eggs appear empty, with only a shadow of the yolk suspended inside. You'll spy a spider-like clump of dark tissue in fertile eggs: a glob with blood vessels radiating out from it like spokes. "Dead germs" are eggs that were fertile but have died; in such eggs, a faint blood ring circles the embryo. If you're not certain you're seeing one, return the egg to the incubator; you can catch it next time.

White eggs are easier to work with than brown or speckled ones, and the second candling is trickier than the first. Is that embryo alive or not? It can be hard for a newbie to tell. Check for candling topics at the Web sites listed in the resources section.

Mark the eggs with an X on one side and an O on the other to help ensure even turning. A coding system is quite helpful since the larger the batch, the easier it is to lose track of your turning cycle. Even turning is imperative for a healthy hatch.

can be retrofitted with the feature. This is must-have equipment, especially if you can't be there to turn the eggs yourself.

Candling Eggs

Candling doesn't harm the growing embryos as long as you work quickly.

Most folks candle eggs at seven days and again one week later. You'll need a dark room and a candling device. These can cost less than $20 (for a basic handheld model) to $350 or more. But for incubator newbies, a homemade version works nicely indeed. Turn out the

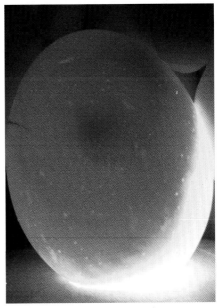

Here is an egg being candled at day seven. Note the embryo's U-shaped shadow and dark eyeball.

Incubation Troubleshooting

Problem	Possible cause
No embryonic development (infertiles)	1) Not enough roosters 2) Aged rooster(s) 3) Temporarily infertile rooster(s) due to frozen comb and wattles 4) Eggs stored too long or incorrectly
Blood rings ("dead germs"); Early embryonic death	1) Incorrect or fluctuating temperatures 2) Eggs stored too long or incorrectly
Many dead early stage embryos	1) Incorrect or fluctuating temperatures (usually too high) 2) Insufficient ventilation 3) Improper egg turning
Fully formed chicks/embryos died before pipping	1) Incorrect temperature 2) Insufficient humidity 3) Insufficient ventilation 4) Improper egg turning 5) Eggs chilled prior to incubation
Fully formed chicks/embryos died during pipping	1) Insufficient humidity 2) Insufficient ventilation 3) Improperly positioned eggs resulting in malpositioned chicks
Early hatch	High temperature
Late or uneven hatch	1) Low temperature 2) Uneven temperature in incubator 3) Old or improperly stored eggs
Chicks stuck to shells	1) Humidity too high during early incubation 2) Humidity too low during late incubation (especially during the three days of hatch)
Crippled chicks	1) Incorrect temperature (usually too high) 2) Low humidity 3) Improper egg turning 4) Insufficient traction on hatching tray
Small, abnormal, or weak chicks	1) Small eggs hatch small chicks 2) High temperature or low humidity 3) Insufficient ventilation 4) Diseased breeder flock 5) Poorly nourished breeder flock
Large, mushy, weak chicks	1) Low temperature 2) Insufficient ventilation
Rough or unhealed navels	High or fluctuating temperatures

What to do

1) Add more roosters
2) Add younger roosters
3) Provide warmer lodgings in midwinter; add fertile roosters to the flock
4) Correct improper storage methods

---

1) Monitor temperature readings more closely
2) Correct improper storage methods

---

1) Monitor temperature readings more closely
2) Increase ventilation/air circulation
3) Turn at least three times a day

---

1) Monitor temperature readings more closely
2) Monitor hygrometer readings more closely
3) Increase ventilation/air circulation
4) Turn at least three times a day
5) Gather eggs often; correct improper storage methods

---

1) Monitor hygrometer readings more closely
2) Boost ventilation/air circulation
3) Set eggs small end down. Don't turn them during the last three days of incubation

---

Operate at recommended temperature; check accuracy of thermometer(s); move incubator to a cooler room

---

1) Operate at recommended temperature; check thermometer's accuracy
2) Contact incubator company for repair or replacement
3) Correct improper storage methods

For both: monitor hygrometer readings more closely

---

1) Monitor thermometer readings more closely
2) Monitor hygrometer readings more closely
3) Turn at least three times a day
4) Use wire floor trays or cover existing tray with cheesecloth

---

1) Discard small hatching eggs
2) Monitor thermometer and hygrometer readings more closely
3) Increase ventilation as needed
4) Use eggs from disease-free flocks
5) Boost flock nutrition

---

1) Monitor thermometer readings more closely
2) Increase ventilation/air circulation

Monitor temperature readings more closely

Incubating Timetable: Preparation to Pipping

First you should buy or collect hatching eggs. Two days prior to setting them, scrub the incubator squeaky clean. Use a weak bleach solution or a commercial product to disinfect the unit and all supplies. Haul the incubator to the spot where it will be parked for the twenty-one-day hatch cycle, then fire it up.

Spend the next two days (or more) fiddling with heat and humidity levels until everything is perfect.

Six hours before you plan to set them, remove your hatching eggs from storage and allow them to come slowly to room temperature. Once incubation commences, religiously monitor conditions inside the unit. Make minor adjustments as needed. Turn the eggs at least three times a day, but don't open the incubator any longer or more often than you absolutely have to. Candle the eggs on days seven and fourteen. Discard the ones you're reasonably certain won't hatch.

Three days prior to the expected hatch (on the eighteenth day of incubation), turn the eggs for the final time, then crank up the heat and humidity. Don't open the incubator again until the hatch is complete. One day before the hatch, clean and disinfect pre-used chick waterers and feeders. Set up your brooder and switch on the heat.

When pipping begins, don't help chicks out of their shells. Opening the incubator compromises the rest of the hatch and a chick who can't break free is nearly always crippled or too weak to survive. Make sure to leave the chicks in the incubator for at least twenty-four hours; certainly until they're fluffy and dry. Taking them out early subjects them to chills. After twenty-four to thirty-six hours, remove the chicks to a warm box and carry them to their brooder.

Hold remaining eggs to your ear and listen closely. If they're going to hatch, you'll hear movement and possibly cheeping; put those eggs back in the incubator and discard the rest of the unhatched eggs. When the hatch is complete, disassemble, scrub, and thoroughly disinfect the incubator and its accessories before packing them away.

Chicks the Old-Fashioned Way

A cheaper and easier way—and often a more successful one—is to hatch eggs under a broody hen. Not all hens brood eggs and none of them do it all the time.

Broodiness by Breed*

Broody
Araucana, Ameraucana, Australorp, Belgian d'Uccle, Brahma, Chanteclar, Cochin, Cubalaya, Dominique, Java, Langshan, Old English Game, Orpington, Silkie, Sumatra, Sussex, Wyandotte

Largely Non-Broody
All hybrid layers and Ancona, Andalusian, Campine, Hamburg, Houdan, Leghorn, Minorca, Spanish White Face

Not every individual of any breed behaves absolutely true to form. The rarest of Silkies will run screaming from nest eggs, while a few hybrid layers will sit.

Because a setting hen lays no eggs and won't lay again for awhile after she hatches chicks, broodiness has been bred out. For example, Leghorns and Leghorn crossbred super-layers almost never brood. At the other end of the spectrum, some Silkie and Cochin bantam hens set and hatch chicks at the drop of a hat. Most bantam, dual-purpose and heavy breed hens (especially Asiatics such as Brahmas and Cochins) will set; Mediterranean and Continental breeds don't often tend to brood.

THE HEN

If a hen lingers in a nest box after laying, if she ruffles her feathers and sputters when you take her egg, lift her off the nest and set her on the floor. Check on her later. If she's on the throne again, you've probably got a broody in the making.

She can set on the eggs she's accumulated if you allow it, or on eggs of your choosing, but you shouldn't let her set them in the henhouse, because other chickens will pick on her. And if she leaves her nest for her daily constitutional and returns to find an interloper on her eggs, there will be a brawl—eggs can be shattered and the broody might lose. It's best to set her up in her own private lodging.

Hens prefer cozy, secluded cubbyholes in which to set. Build your broody a disposable getaway by slicing ventilation slots that are 1 inch from the tops of all four sides of a lidded cardboard box that is slightly larger than hen. Generously pad the bottom with chopped wheat straw or shavings.

Hollow out a bowl-shaped depression in the nesting material, and then wait until dark to relocate your hen. When you do, wear gloves—she'll peck, *hard*!

Reach under the hen and remove her eggs. Nestle them into the broody box nesting material, then move the hen. Slide your hand beneath her, fingers facing up; wait until she quits fussing and settles down onto your palm. Then transfer her to her temporary home and close the lid.

Place the box in a predator-proof, dimly lit spot. Get a small, deep container of water and cuddle it into the litter in one corner of the box; place a shallow bowl of feed in another (soup and tuna cans work well). Don't open the lid again until late the following day. This will give your hen time to acclimate to her new home, and she'll appreciate the solitude during this period. She will have food and drink if

Power Outages

If your power goes out, don't abandon the hatch. Carry your incubator to the warmest place in your house. If it's a forced air model, crack the lid to admit fresh air; it's better to keep still air models closed.

Should the power come on within a few hours, resume incubation but candle the clutch four to six days later and discard any eggs that appear to have died. Surviving eggs require more time to hatch, sometimes as much as one or two days.

If 50 percent of the eggs you set hatch, celebrate! A lot can go wrong during the home incubation process; a 50/50 hatch is a good one, indeed.

John just removed Gracie from her nest and she's furious. His thick gloves are more than a precautionary measure; an enraged broody hen will surely peck at the hands invading her space.

she wants it (she probably won't, but giving her the option will make you feel better), and she won't mess her nest just because she can't get out. If she seems content, cut an entryway in one side of her haven, then pat your back: you've successfully resettled a hen!

Once she begins setting, a hen's physiology changes. Her temperature drops to around 100 degrees, and her metabolism slows. She molts feathers from her breast and underpinnings, the better for her skin to warm eggs and later, chicks (the molted feathers would act as insulation if she didn't lose them). She remains on her eggs, feathers ruffled and wings slightly extended to warm them, full-time until they hatch, save a half hour or so every day or two to drink, grab a bite to eat, and make 'broody poop' (a memorably stinky, single, gigantic glob of birdy-doo).

She'll sit until her chickies hatch or it's obvious that they won't. If she's still setting on unhatched eggs after twenty-three days, day-old hatchery chicks or another hen's newly-hatched babies can be fostered under her. Salt her nest with chickies at night; by morning, chances are she'll decide they're her very own.

THE NEW CHICKS

Don't allow a hen with brand new chicks to free range or to immediately rejoin the main flock. Other chickens may harry her or the babies and when the little ones trail mama through wet grass, they easily chill. Chilled peeps are likely to die. Cats, hawks, skunks, and their kind adore chickie aperitifs, so if you want them to live, house those chicks and their mama in their own separate coop.

Babies should be fed a chick-starter ration inside of a creep feeder. This is a structure only they can enter, because its openings are too tiny for mama to squeeze through. An over-

This little guy is the first of his clutch to pip, and the neighboring eggs aren't far behind. Avoid the urge to help a pipping chick out of his shell. If he lacks the strength to emerge, he won't be suited for life on the farm.

turned heavyweight cardboard box with chick-size openings carved into its sides makes a fine, free creep feeder. Weight the box top with a brick or flat stone just heavy enough to keep mama from tipping it over.

Make certain the peeps can always reach fresh water. Place a chick waterer in the brooder pen. Drop some marbles into the drinking surface to prevent the chicks from drowning, and keep it clean.

When they're a month old and nicely started, the chicks and their mama can join the flock. But monitor things for awhile; some adult chickens are mean to another hen's chicks.

Hatching Eggs 101

Whether you hatch chicks under a real, live mama or inside a "tin hen," you'll want to begin with quality eggs. Following are several requirements for quality eggs.

Fertile. Hens don't need a rooster's input to lay eggs, but if you want fertile eggs, you definitely need the services of Mr. Roo. He shouldn't be too young—or too old; he also should be actively breeding hens. You need one prime rooster for every eighteen bantam, twelve light-breed, or eight heavy hens in your flock.

Clean. A poop-smeared egg can spread fecal-borne disease to the embryo within and to other, cleaner eggs in the clutch. Scrubbing won't help. Bathing removes the protective natural sealant present on newly-laid eggs and is apt to force bacteria through the egg's porous shell. Some folks lightly sand away splots with finest-grain sandpaper, while others believe that doing so weakens the shell. Is it worth the risk? Probably not, especially if other, cleaner eggs are available.

Average size. Huge eggs don't hatch well; undersized eggs hatch undersized chicks. An average size is best.

"Egg shaped" and intact. Toss cracked eggs, misshapen eggs, and any with shells that are wrinkled, rough-textured, or thinner than usual.

Promptly gathered. Collect hatching eggs first thing every morning and recheck nests throughout the day. Don't let them get chilled, overheated, or unnecessarily soiled due to being in the nest too long.

Properly stored. Fertile hatching eggs should be placed in egg cartons, small end down, and tilted to one side, then stored in a cool (50-60 degrees), humid (70-75 percent) place in your house. Never keep hatching eggs in the refrigerator! A simple way to turn them (you only need to do this once a day) is to slip a 1-inch slice of a 2-by-4 under one end of the carton, then move it to the opposite end the next day. Keep it up until you're ready to set the eggs. Don't store them longer than ten days—and less is a whole lot better.

WHEN YOU DON'T WANT CHICKS

Not everyone wants their hens to brood. Setting hens, hens raising their chicks, and post-broody hens who didn't hatch a brood (because their eggs were infertile, a predator snatched them, or for any other reason) don't lay eggs. And the longer she broods, the longer the interval before she'll lay again.

Furthermore, not every hen makes the very best mom. Some abandon their nests mid-incubation, while others are so scattered, they stomp on and shatter their eggs. Less maternal souls sometimes hatch their brood successfully but dislike their chicks; they'll peck their chicks' little noggins—and worse—some kill their babies (and eat them!).

Free spirit hens gallivant off and leave their babes to their own devices. Whatever causes these hens to behave this way, they shouldn't be allowed to set eggs, unless you're willing to snatch their newly-hatched chicks and raise the peeps in a brooder.

These babies stay close by their mama's side. Wait at least a month before allowing a hen and her chicks to join the main flock to avoid possible scuffles between veterans and the youngsters.

These young birds from Gib and Melba Mullins' Missouri farm aren't quite old enough to leave their brooder box to join the rest of the flock. A brooder provides a warm environment for newly hatched chicks to grow during their first month.

If you want to turn your broody hen's mind to laying instead of hatching chicks, you have to "break her up." Breaking up a broody sounds easy—just cart her eggs away and off she goes—but it's not; most broodies continue setting, eggs or not. And sometimes it goes on for a good, long (nonproductive) time.

If you've removed her eggs but your hen stoutly insists on setting, try some proven ploys to get her to stop. First, after nightfall, pull on your gloves, hoist Ms. Broody up out of her nest, and resettle her in a completely new location for three or four days (or more, if needed).

Disassemble the nest before you release her. If it's disposable, toss it. If she was holed up in one of your laying nests and you moved it for her, scrub and disinfect it, refill it with fresh nesting material, and take it back to the henhouse where it belongs.

If that doesn't work, try temporarily housing her in a "broody coop," a wire mesh cage (a small all-wire rabbit hutch works well) suspended from the roof or a rafter, where cool air circulating around the hen's torrid underpinnings is likely to break through her single-minded trace. One caveat: make certain you don't hang her in a draft! Three or four days in the broody coop should work its magic. Placing two handfuls of ice cubes under her several times a day or bathing her in cold (but not icy) water then carting her off to short-term incarceration should also speed along the process and cool her underpinnings, too.

Whatever you try, persevere: you can outlast a hen! Provide her with plenty of food and water, despite what a few old-timers may tell you. Most seasoned chicken keepers claim starving broodies makes them surrender sooner but starving her will weaken an already stressed bird, and she may even die.

To discourage hens from going broody in the first place, choose a breed that doesn't tend to set. Promptly remove fresh eggs from nest boxes; encountering an inviting collection of eggs triggers the urge to brood in many good hens of the broodier breeds.

BROODING PEEPS

So now you have chicks. Whether from a hatchery, your incubator, or out from under a hen, they're yours to raise. It can be tricky but if you stick to the rules, brooding peeps isn't hard. To have fun doing it and to lose fewer chicks, here's what you have to know.

THE BROODER

If there is a brooder house on your farm, fine and dandy. If it hasn't been cleaned since its last occupation, strip the floors and disinfect them. Sweep down cobwebs and disinfect the lower walls, too.

Decide where to hang your heat lamp (more about this later) and erect a cardboard draft protection shield beneath it. Use a commercial product (mail-order hatcheries and poultry supply houses sell them) or a homemade version fashioned from 12-18 inches high panels snipped from cardboard boxes and connected with strips of duct tape. A 6-foot circle is fine for fifty chicks; if you have fewer than that, it's easier to brood in a box and transfer chicks to the floor later on.

This basket of brown eggs is picture perfect! Check on your hens several times a day—eggs that sit too long in the hen house have more opportunity to become soiled.

Marge takes shelter in a ventilated crate in our daytime enclosure, but at nearly 90 degrees she's still hot and panting. Some hens will continue to set even after you have removed their eggs. To put a stop to their unproductive setting, carefully remove the stubborn birds and disassemble the nests.

Most small-scale chicken raisers don't own brooder houses. Initially, it doesn't matter. Today's favorite chick brooder is a secondhand cardboard box stowed in your home in a warm, out-of-the-way spot. A semi-topless cardboard box (leave the flaps on so you can regulate ventilation) is clean, dry, and draft free. When the chicks outgrow it or it gets smelly, simply dispose of it.

Transfer the chickies to a new box and shred the old one for the compost pile. Nothing could be simpler!

Other ingenious homemade brooders can be fashioned of flexible plastic wading pools, old aquariums, dog crates, or rabbit hutches fitted with cardboard draft shields. Our personal favorite: inexpensive plastic storage box brooders like this one.

Or you can always buy a ready-made brooder. A traditional galvanized steel box-type model with mesh floor, built-in water and feed troughs, and its own heating unit costs in the neighborhood of $200 and houses fifty chicks for up to fourteen days.

Stromberg's plastic brooder, which has a twelve-chick capacity and is made of high-impact plastic, is a better bet for pet and small flock owners. It resembles an airline pet carrier, breaks down easily for cleaning, and heats nicely with a 75- to 150-watt incandescent lightbulb. At less than $35 postpaid, it's a steal!

THE FURNISHINGS

Whichever type of brooder you have, you'll need to furnish it with a heat source, litter, feeders, and waterers. Consider the following when choosing which kinds to buy.

Heat Sources

Ready-made brooders usually incorporate their own heaters. If yours doesn't, or if

Brooder Requirements

Age	Temperature	Floor space per chick	Waterer space per chick	Feeder space per chick
Week 1	95 °F.	3 sq. in.	.50 in.	1 in.
Week 2-3	90°F–85°F	6 sq. in.	.50 in.	1.50 in.
Week 4-5	80°F–75°F	9 sq. in.	.75 in.	2 in.
Week 6-8	70°F (Higher if chicks seem chilly)	1 sq. ft.	.75 in.	2 in.

your brooder is the homemade kind, you'll need a reliable heat lamp to warm those tender chickies or they won't survive.

Infrared heat lamps, which come in clear and red bulb versions, provide the constant heat that wee chicks require. Red bulbs throw less light and are said to prevent juvenile picking that sometimes leads to cannibalism (we'll discuss this charming habit in a bit). When choosing an infrared lamp, opt for a UL-approved model with a porcelain socket and a lamp guard. If reusing an older unit, make certain its cord hasn't frayed.

Used improperly, these lamps can burn down barns, brooder houses, and homes, so make absolutely certain the lamp can't fall or overheat nearby flammable surfaces. Hang it by a chain, not by its cord! You'll need one lamp fitted with a 75- to 150-watt bulb per fifty to seventy-five peeps.

Storage box and aquarium brooders can be heated with everyday lightbulbs. You'll need a variety of wattages in the 75-watt range in order to adjust the temperature. A gooseneck table light makes a handy fixture for tabletop brooders. Whichever type your heating unit requires, don't forget to buy extra bulbs!

Litter

The litter you choose makes a world of difference. It must be insulative, absorbent, and provide lots of grip. Lodging new chicks on slick sheets of newsprint or flattened cardboard makes their tiny legs slip to the sides, causing **spraddle leg**. Spraddle-legged chicks can sometimes be salvaged by hobbling them with Band-Aids or makeup sponges until their legs correct, but spraddle leg is a problem better prevented than cured.

Sawdust sometimes confuses new chicks, who think it's food. Ingested sawdust leads to **pasty butt**—droppings stuck to a tiny chickie's tush. If you don't soak or pick it off, the chick can't eliminate and he'll quickly die. Sawdust litter should not be used until chicks are a few weeks old.

First-class litter materials include pine shavings, coarsely ground corn-

A utility lamp provides essential heat for these newborns. Store-bought brooder boxes may come with a heat source, but homemade versions will require a bit of creativity. Be sure your choice is securely fastened and is of the correct wattage to prevent injury or death.

cobs or peanut shells, rice hulls, peat moss, sand, and old bath towels weighted down at the corners and laundered whenever they get soiled. Don't use hardwood shavings; some species are toxic to tiny chicks.

Initially bed the brooder area with 3-6 inches of litter, more if it's chilly outdoors and the brooder sets directly on a floor. Stir and fluff litter every day. Scoop water spills and messes as they occur. Add bedding whenever needed to keep things cozy and tidy.

Feeders

Flying saucer-shaped galvanized steel feeders with hole-studded snap-top lids are ideal for tabletop brooders. Folks with more chicks to brood will probably prefer trough feeders, (allowing 2 feet of feeder per each twenty-four chicks).

Empty pressed-fiber egg cartons make feeders for tiny chicks that are both easily accessible and disposable, although they'll climb on and poop in them, wasting a lot of feed in the process.

If you're raising meat chicks, choose 20-22 percent protein broiler starter for them; if they are pets or future layers, standard 18-20 percent protein chick starter is a wiser choice.

Most starters are medicated with Amprolium to prevent coccidiosis until the chicks develop their own immunity to this common disease. Some feed is

The rocks in this waterer prevent tiny chicks from drowning. This model contains electrolyte- and vitamin-laced water, which gives baby birds a jump start on proper nutrition.

While this mason jar can hold a lot of feed, we only fill it halfway at most. Chickens bill out excess feed and spoil it by soiling in it and walking on it. Over time, their wastefulness adds up to a lot of unnecessary expense.

laced with antibiotics, too. Non-medicated feed is available, but you'll have to ask for it—and likely pay a premium price—if you want it.

Unless you supplement your chicks' diet with scratch, they won't require grit. If you do choose to supplement the food, buy special chick grit or cage bird grit (available from a pet store).

Waterers

If your brood is a small one, you'll need one plastic-based quart canning jar waterer for each dozen chicks. For larger broods, one gallon-size waterer services fifty chicks. Chicks easily drown in waterers, so whichever type you choose, add marbles or pebbles until only their beaks can get wet. When you place units in the brooder, don't position any near the heat source; chicks don't fancy warm water and might not drink at all if it's hot. Empty and brush-scrub waterers every day; rinse them with a weak bleach solution once a week. Make certain waterers are filled and functional at all times.

Many veteran chicken raisers spike peeps' drinking water with table sugar (one-quarter cup sugar per gallon of water) to give them a needed energy boost. Others

These Silkie and Old English game chicks snack on scrambled egg yolks.

swear by vitamin and electrolyte supplements like Murray McMurray Hatchery's Quik-Chik and Broiler Boosters. If you plan to use water supplements, lace the peeps' drinking water right from the start.

PUTTING IT ALL TOGETHER

At least twenty-four hours before anticipated hatch or delivery, set up your brooder, switch on the heat lamp, and bring everything up to heat. The temperature at chick height (2-3 inches from the floor) must run a constant 95 degrees for the first full week; use a thermometer to check it twice a day. You'll lower the temperature by about 5 degrees each week until the chicks are five weeks old. After that, maintaining heat at 70 degrees (or indoor room temperature) generally does the trick.

Chicks instinctively pick at whatever they see, so for the first few days, carpet their litter with nubby paper towels. Sprinkle a thin layer of chick starter on it to encourage the chicks to pick at feed instead of litter. Tempt slow learning chicks with chopped boiled egg yolk sprinkled on paper towels or drizzled atop their regular feed. Egg yolk is the ideal chickie appetizer!

Examine New Arrivals

Remove chicks from their shipping box one by one and examine them. If the chick has pasty butt (as is common with

Tiny Incubator Can Due!

I hatched our Li'l Due in a $15 incubator. I started with three eggs, but he was the only one who hatched. I had to help him from the shell, and he had splayed legs, but I put an adhesive bandage on them, and he only had to wear it one day until he was fine. He's almost ten months old now. The little incubators do work.

I had to keep the room at a steady temperature, though. If the room got warmer, so did the incubator. All I had was the little thermometer that came with it and the little plastic wrap reflectors. I didn't have a water weasel; I just kept the feet filled with water in the incubator. It may have been beginner's luck, and there was certainly a lot of prayer involved, too!

—*Patty Mousty, New Albany, IN*

No Incubator?

I think it would be better for new chicken people to buy chicks. There are many things that can go wrong when you incubate and that could discourage a new chicken owner. They have spent a lot of money and will never use the incubator again.

Chicks are cheap, you can get them sexed or sexed links, and you are going to get the right number or close to the right number. Brooder box management is hard enough to start with. Start with the cute fuzzys, then do eggs. After you have chickens awhile, then you can decide if you want to incubate.

—*Helen Jenson, Silverton, OR*

Treasure That Hen

When you find a hen who likes to hatch eggs and does a good job of it, guard her with your life! You can set Guinea eggs, ducks eggs, even goose eggs under her if she's big enough. Ducks or geese with a chicken mom are such fun. It drives the chicken mom crazy when her chicks make a beeline for mud puddles!

—*Marci Roberts, Springfield, MO*

Can't tell chicks apart? We mark ours with a non-toxic ink pen or food coloring. Don't use red—chicks instinctively pick at it.

mail-order chicks, especially in their first five or six days after arrival), gently wash his little behind with a soft cloth dampened in warm water. Check the toes.

Caught early, crooked or curled toes can be splinted using wooden match sticks and strips of adhesive bandage snipped to size. Some straighten, some don't, but you won't know unless you try! If a chick looks normal, dip his beak in water so he knows where it is and he starts drinking, and then place the bird gently under the heat source.

Listen and Look

Listen to your chicks. Contented chicks converse in gentle cheeps; frantic, shrill peeping means they're chilly. Up the heat by moving the lamp closer to the chicks or substitute a higher wattage bulb. Keep an eye on your chicks, too.

Happy chicks spread throughout the brooder, allowing each other plenty of space. Chilled chicks cluster beneath the heat source, sometimes piling atop one another and suffocating the babes at the bottom of the heap. Overheated chicks extend their teensy wings and pant; they flock to the outer edges of the brooder to flee excessive heat. When the peeps huddle at one side of the heat lamp or another, suspect a draft.

Ongoing Care

Once chicks are eating well, fill feeders halfway full (to reduce waste), but never let them run out of water or feed. If feed

Tabletop Brooder—*It's a Good One!*

To make your own tabletop brooder, you will need:

- A hard plastic storage box, preferably with translucent sides. You'll find a huge variety to choose from at Target or Wal-Mart. Figure necessary floor space per chick before you go shopping. If one box isn't enough to house them through the brooding period, start out with all the chicks in one, then transfer part to another box as the brood matures. You can count on the following space requirements per chick: Through the end of week three: 6 sq. in. Weeks four through five: 9 sq. in. Weeks six through eight: 1 sq. ft.
- A sharp knife (an Exacto knife works well)
- 1/4 inch mesh hardware cloth A piece slightly smaller than the box's lid.
- 10 bolts, 1/4 by 1/2 inches in length; washers and nuts for each (this may vary depending on lid design)
- A sharp nail or awl to use as a scribe
- Wire snips, a drill, and a screwdriver

First, invert the box top on a hard surface. Scribe a 1-inch border inside any framed panels (some lids feature a single panel, others two). Using the sharp knife, cut a window or windows into the lid. Allowing a 1-inch overlap, snip the hardware cloth screen to fit, drill holes to secure it, and bolt it down. That's it!

Place a gooseneck reading lamp on the screen to use as a brooder lamp. Fiddle with standard lightbulbs of various wattages until the interior temperature is perfect. Fine-tune temperatures by raising or lowering the lamp. Switch to hotter or cooler light bulbs if needed. Nothing could be easier!

Use our easy plans to build this translucent plastic box brooder.

gets damp or dirty, dump it; rinse and dry the feeder before replenishing it with fresh starter.

Carefully and frequently handle future pets, but for only a few minutes at a time; otherwise it's best to leave tiny chicks in the brooder. Supervise children; remind them that the peeps are fragile, and make certain kids wash their hands after handling chicks.

Nip toe and feather picking in the bud. Chicks pick each other when they're too hot, too crowded, when their light is too bright, if the air is too stale, or their feed inadequate, or sometimes simply because they feel like it. Picking leads to cannibalism—not a pretty sight.

Chicks instinctively peck at everything in their environment, so if yours begin picking one another, add grass clippings to their diet. Strew bits of healthful greenery around the floor and let them pick at that, giving the chickies something constructive to do. Switch the clear heat lamp or lightbulb for a red one.

Remove picked chicks to safer quarters and dab their wounds with anti-pick solution, such as Hot Pick, Blue Kote, or an old favorite, pine tar, to heal them and deter further picking.

As chicks mature, provide additional floor space, feeders, and waterers. If brooding in a brooder house, remove the draft shield when the chicks are three weeks old. By the time they're six weeks old, chicks are fully feathered and fit to face the world. It's time to move pullets to the henhouse and meat chickens to quarters of their own.

This handsome White Rock pullet takes a cautious spin around the great outdoors on her first foray outside the chicken yard. It's best not to free range chickens until they're five or six months old.

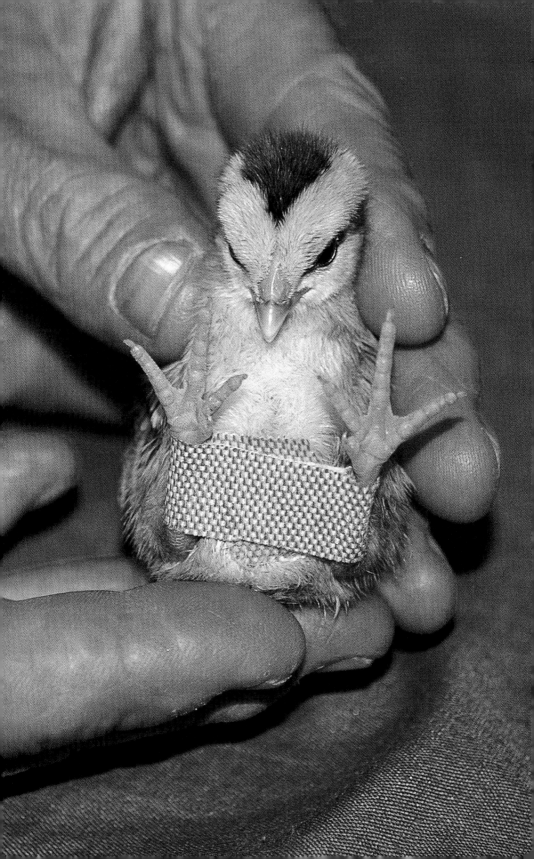

CHAPTER SIX

Chickens as Patients

M ost introductory chicken manuals fail in their attempt to describe the thousand and one diseases, maladies, and afflictions that sometimes befall our friend, the chicken. This one isn't even going to try. The amount of information we could pack between these pages would be scant indeed, compared with the plethora of readily accessible, specialty material available on the Internet. Check out the resources in the back of this book, print what interests you and stuff your printouts in a binder: create your own poultry veterinary book.

PREVENTING PROBLEMS

It's infinitely easier to keep chickens healthy than to doctor them after the fact, and in most cases, keeping them healthy isn't at all hard. To keep healthy, happy, bright-eyed chickens begin with healthy, happy, bright-eyed chickens.

Buy from reliable sources; don't stock your coop with someone else's rejects or bedraggled bargain fowl picked up at country swap meets.

Consider starting with day-old chicks from reputable hatcheries and what you're working with right from the get-go. Maintain a closed flock. Don't indiscriminately add chickens to your collection. It upsets the flock's hierarchy and causes infighting and stress. It's also the best possible way to introduce disease.

Provide suitable quarters. They needn't be fancy, but they must be clean, roomy, well-ventilated, and draft free. Feed your chickens what they need to thrive. Keep plenty of sparkling clean drinking water available. Furnish enough feeders and waterers to make certain every chicken can eat or drink whenever he or she pleases.

Avoid unnecessary stresses. For example, don't let your kids or dog chase the chickens, handle them gently, make changes gradually, and don't upset the status quo. Laid-back chickens tend to be healthy chickens; keeping them happy will keep disease at bay.

It's important to recognize problems early, while they're still fairly simple to fix. Consult the Is My Chicken Healthy chart for general signs of health and ill health.

MALADIES: PARASITES AND DISEASES

A parasite-savvy chicken raiser knows early detection is a key to keeping chickens healthy. Most chickens are exposed to wild birds, which commonly spread parasites and disease. Left unchecked, parasites can spread like wildfire through your flock, causing anemia, weight loss, decreased egg production, and even death.

PARASITES, LICE, AND MITES

Chickens sometimes do have worms. Zap external and internal parasites before they cause problems. However, don't rely on over-the-counter remedies that treat parasites your chickens might not have. Instead, collect a community fecal sample using material from a number of chicken plops and take it to your vet to be checked for worm eggs. If worms are present, she'll prescribe a wormer custom tailored for your flock. Do this twice a year to keep your birds in the pink

Lice and mites are the scourge of the henhouse, and you need to be vigilant and take care of them. The first step is to know what you're dealing with. See the Chicken Itchies chart for a description of the big four.

For the scoop on external creepies, scope out the University of Florida's bulletin, "External Parasites of Poultry" at

This Black Jersey Giant has horribly twisted toes, a defect with both dietary and genetic roots.

Is My Chicken Healthy?

What to Check	Healthy	Unhealthy
Temperature	103°F–103.5°F.	Higher/lower
Respiration	Easy, even	Labored, rasping, coughing
Posture	Stands erect, head and tail elevated; alert and active	Hunkered down, tail and wings drooping; depressed
Appetite	Eats often	Uninterested in food
Thirst	Drinks often	Excessive thirst
Manure	Formed mass, gray to brown with white caps; fecal droppings may be frothy	Liquid or sticky; green, yellow, white, red
Condition	Feels heavy, firm, powerful	Thin, weak, thin-breasted
Feathers	Smooth, neat, clean	Ruffled or broken, dirty, stained
Comb and Wattles	Bright red; firm	Shrunken, pale, or blue
Eyes	Bright and alert	Dull, watery, possibly partially closed
Nostrils	Clean	Crusty, caked
Legs and Feet	Plump, scales clean and waxy smooth, warm joints	Enlarged, crusty scales; hot, swollen joints; Soles of feet crusty, cracked, or discolored

http://edis.ifas.ufl.edu/BODY_IG140. Before applying any commercial bug blaster, read the label carefully and follow instructions exactly—or refer to the detailed formulation, mixing and application instructions in the University of Georgia publication, "Poultry External Parasite Control" available at http://www.ent.uga.edu/pmh/Animals/poultry_parasite.htm.

COMMUNICABLE POULTRY DISEASES: THE BIG, SCARY ONES

It's unlikely your pet chicken or small farm flock will succumb to one of the big, exotic poultry diseases currently in the news. However, these diseases are out there, so you need to be able to recognize their symptoms. If you do suspect one such disease has a toehold in your flock, bring in the big guns. Most of these are diseases that must be reported to health authorities, and it's your duty to wave the red flag. (See the Major Chicken Maladies chart for a summary of the diseases listed below.)

Avian Influenza: Avian influenza is a highly contagious respiratory infection caused by type A influenza orthomyxoviruses. Symptoms vary widely and range from mild to serious. Death occurs

Chicken Itchies

Poultry Lice

While there are many forms of poultry lice, the most common are the chicken body louse *(Menacanthus stramineus)* and the shaft louse *(Manopan gallinae)*.

- Fast-moving, 6-legged, flat-bodied insect with broad, round head; 2-3 mm long, straw-colored (light brown).
- Female lays 50 to 300 tiny white eggs near base of feather shafts.
- Does not suck blood; feeds on dry skin scales, feathers, scabs; gives infested birds a moth-eaten look.
- Spends entire life cycle on host.
- Its primary infestation season is fall and winter.
- Dust or spray birds and their environment using commercial products containing Malathion, Permethrin, Rabon, or Sevin, carefully following the instructions on the label. Always consult with your veterinarian before use.

Chicken Mite (also called Red Roost Mite)
Dermanyssus gallinae

- Slow-moving, 8-legged insect; 1 mm long (the size of coarsely ground pepper); gray to dark reddish brown.
- Lays white or off-white eggs on fluff feathers and along larger feather shafts.
- Sucks blood only at night; hides in cracks and crevices in coop or poultry building during the day.
- Its primary infestation season is summer.
- Dust or spray birds and their environment using commercial products containing Malathion, Permethrin, Rabon, or Sevin, carefully following the instructions on the label. Always consult with your veterinarian before use.

Northern Fowl Mite
Ornithonyssus sylviarum

- Slow-moving, 8-legged insect; 1 mm long (the size of coarsely ground pepper); brown.
- Lays white or off-white eggs on fluff feathers and along larger feather shafts located on host's vent, tail, back, and neck.
- Sucks blood.
- Spends entire life cycle on host; feeds day or night.
- Its primary infestation seasons are fall, winter, and spring
- Dust or spray birds and their environment using commercial products containing Malathion, Permethrin, Rabon, or Sevin, carefully following the instructions on the label. Always consult with your veterinarian before use.

Scaly Leg Mite
Knemidokoptes mutans

- Slow-moving, 8-legged insect; 1 mm long; gray
- Sucks blood.
- Burrows into and lives under the scales of the feet, causing lifting and separation from underlying skin. Results in swelling, tenderness, scabbing, and deformity. Related joint problems may occur.
- Coating the entire leg shaft with petroleum jelly or vegetable, mineral, or linseed oil every two days may help smooth and moisturize scales.
- Dust or spray birds, coop, and roosts with carbaryl products such as Sevin, carefully following the instructions on the label. Always consult with your veterinarian before use.
- Ivermectin pour-on (also called spot-on) is a systemic agent used to control both internal and external parasites.

A White Rock rooster peeks out from the bushes. His waxy comb and wattles are a sign of his good health.

suddenly; the disease sweeps through a flock in just one to three days. Avian influenza occurs in many forms worldwide and in the United States must be reported.

Fowl Cholera: Fowl cholera is an acute, relatively common disease caused by *Pasteurella multocida* bacteria. It spreads rapidly and kills quickly; chickens die within hours after symptoms appear. Humans handling infected birds sometimes contract upper respiratory infections.

Infectious Coryza: Infectious coryza is found worldwide; in the United States, most cases occur in the southeastern states and California. A respiratory infection caused by *Haemophilus paragallinarum* bacteria, coryza often manifests in combination with other chronic respiratory diseases. While contagious, it usually isn't fatal.

Infectious Bronchitis: Infectious bronchitis is a common, fast-spreading, and highly contagious respiratory disease

Major Chicken Maladies

Disease	Symptoms
Avian Influenza (Virus)	Mild form: coughing, sneezing, decline in egg production
Fowl Cholera (Bacterium)	Systemic form: chronic respiratory infection, high mortality
Infectious Coryza (Bacterial)	Green diarrhea, darkened head and comb, swollen feet, paralysis, swollen wattles, listlessness, high mortality
Infectious Bronchitis (Virus)	Watery eyes, putrid nasal discharge, swollen face and wattles, sneezing
Fowl Pox (Virus)	Coughing, sneezing, gasping, nasal discharge, respiratory distress, depression, marked drop in egg production
Infectious Laryngotracheitis (Virus)	DRY FORM: brownish-yellow lesions on the unfeathered skin of the head, neck, legs, and feet. WET FORM: labored breathing, lesions in the mucous membranes of the mouth, tongue, upper digestive tract, and respiratory tract. Reduced egg production; low mortality
Marek's Disease (Virus)	Partial paralysis, blindness, wasting, tumors

Prevention	Comments
Vaccination	A reportable disease spread by people, birds, and flies
Vaccination (but not until cholera has been diagnosed in the flock; even so, vaccination may not be effective); proper sanitation and rodent and predator control; proper disposal of dead birds	Caused by secretions from carrier birds, cannibalism of dead birds, contaminated water, feed, equipment, or clothing
Don't indiscriminately introduce outside birds into your flock; if possible, raise replacements from day-old chicks	Spread by direct bird-to-bird contact and contaminated feed and water; often introduced to the flock by seemingly healthy carrier birds
Vaccination, proper sanitation, quarantine of all new birds	Caused by inhaled airborne respiratory droplets and contaminated food and water; often introduced when non-quarantined new birds are added to a flock
Vaccination	Spread by mosquitoes and ingestion of sloughed scabs
Vaccination	Spread mainly via infected birds' droppings
Vaccination shortly after hatching	Caused by inhalation of virus-laden feather follicle dander. Spread mainly via infected birds' droppings

caused by several strains of coronavirus. While chicks often succumb to the infection, adult chickens generally survive but remain carriers for life.

Fowl Pox: There are two types of fowl pox—wet, sometimes called Avian pox, and dry, also known as fowl diphtheria (Neither is related to human chicken pox). Caused by the same virus and transmitted in the same manner, the former is primarily a skin disease while the latter affects both the skin and the respiratory tract.

Infectious Laryngotracheitis: Infectious laryngotracheitis (sometimes called Avian diptheria) is a slow-spreading, but serious, upper respiratory tract infection caused by a herpes virus. It manifests worldwide and commonly afflicts laying hens during the winter months.

Marek's Disease: Marek's disease is a global scourge; it kills more chickens worldwide than any other disease. Marek's symptoms vary according to its victims' ages but it often culminates in sudden death. Caused by six different herpes viruses, it is virulently contagious. Chicks vaccinated at one day of age are usually immune for life.

Newcastle Disease: Newcastle disease manifests in many forms and in varying degrees of seriousness. It's not generally fatal, and survivors gain immu-

We keep a close eye on these newly hatched Red Jungle Fowl chicks. Put an immediate stop to picking among your young birds—the habit can quickly lead to cannibalism.

First Aid Kit

Be ready for inevitable avian emergencies by assembling a chicken first aid kit. You will need:

- A sturdy container. Supplies for a small flock fit neatly in a large fishing tackle box or a lidded bucket. Keep the container stocked; if you use something, replace the remainder when you're finished or replenish the used stock with a new supply. Store the kit where you can find it quickly. And, write your veterinarian's phone number on the lid with permanent marker (post the number by the telephone, too).

- A flashlight with a strong beam. Tuck it to a zip-lock bag with an extra set of batteries and a fresh bulb

Into a second zip-lock bag, place injury treatment materials such as:
- First aid tape in several widths
- Stretch gauze
- Gauze pads
- Cotton balls
- Wooden Popsicle sticks to use for splints
- To prevent spills and messes, cache medicinals in a third zip-lock bag:

- VetRX Veterinary Remedy for Poultry (for respiratory distress)
- Anti-pick spray or ointment
- Wound powder, herbal wound dressing, antiseptic spray or ointment
- Saline solution for cleaning wounds and injured eyes
- Holistic chicken keepers might add Bach Rescue Remedy (or Cream)
- Any other medicines your veterinarian recommends

A final zip-lock bag contains hardware:
- Scissors
- Dog toenail clippers for snipping nails and beak tips
- One or more 5 cc or larger catheter-tip disposable syringes for feeding and watering debilitated chickens

Add a pet carrier for transporting sick chickens to their vet and a quarantine cage and you'll be set for most any emergency. Put it together now, before you need it. You (and your chickens) will be glad you did.

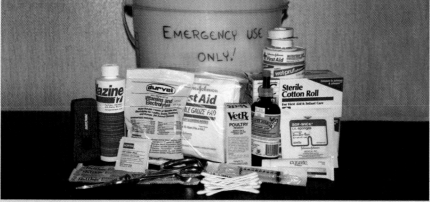

Our first aid kit contains all that we would need to treat an injured bird, from antiseptic ointment to VetRX for respiratory infections.

nity for life. Caused by a paramyxovirus, Newcastle can trigger minor eye infections in humans who handle the live vaccine or infected chickens.

PICKING AND CANNIBALISM

Although not diseases, picking and cannibalism are the most vexing aspects of chicken keeping and clearly major threats to the health of your flock. On occasion, chickens literally peck each other to death. Worse, once it happens, the habit is readily established. It's important to nip this vile habit in the bud with adults and chicks alike.

Cannibalism usually takes root when one of the flock is injured. The sight of blood draws her peers because chickens pick at anything red. Unless the injured chicken is removed, the pecking escalates and she's likely to be pecked until she's dead. Although mildly injured chickens can be left in the flock and treated with commercial products such as Hot Pick to thwart further pecking, it's better to separate them until they've fully recovered. Installed in their own quarters and administered, antibiotic or herbal ointments; healing will be hastened and by rescuing them, you'll likely save their lives. In general, don't leave wounded, lame, weak, undersized, odd-colored, or otherwise unusual birds in a flock of aggressive peers. To preserve their lives, move them to safer quarters.

Many other factors influence cannibalism within a given flock, including overcrowding, intense lighting and heat, diet, breed-related problems, and stress.

Molting and an aggressive rooster are both causes of this hen's (at right) damaged feathers. Relocate a hen who's been the target of a flockmate's aggression to prevent further injury.

A nice hatch of Easter egger chicks have just graduated from their brooder box to this coop with outdoor access. Moving your chickens to a new environment can heighten their stress level. This is a time to keep an extra close watch on behavior.

Address the problems of overcrowding by removing some birds, moving the flock to a roomier coop, or turning them outdoors. You can also install additional waterers, feeders, and nesting boxes. Dim the lights, install fans, and create more shade to prevent the overly high activity level that results from bright lighting and the edginess caused by sizzling, steamy heat. If you suspect that diet is the culprit in negative behavior, try different combinations until you find something that works. For instance, confined, solely scratch-fed chickens sometimes don't receive sufficient nutrients from their diet. If they begin pecking one another, switching to commercial feed or a commercial feed or scratch blend sometimes helps. Conversely, chickens fed a strictly commercial diet sometimes peck out of boredom.

Strewing scratch grains, garden greenery, or acceptable table scraps adds dietary variety and scratching and nibbling at these goodies gives idle chickens something to do. Flighty, nervous birds such as Leghorns, Minorcas, and many other Mediterranean breeds are more likely to pick; circumvent this problem by ruling them out for your farm. Finally, and most fundamentally, avoid situations that will leave your birds stressed like rough handling, temperature extremes, and abrupt changes in routine.

ORGANIC EGGS FOR SALE

BROWN!

$1.20 DOZ.

CHAPTER SEVEN

Farm Fresh Eggs and Finger Lickin' Chicken

W hether you keep chickens for pleasure or for profit, chances are you use or sell their yummy eggs. Raising chickens for meat is a sure way to know exactly what does—and does not—go into your bird before it reaches your table; you'll know the donors were handled humanely and exactly how their eggs or flesh was processed. Homegrown poultry and eggs are infinitely fresher and tastier than anything you can buy in a store, and producing wholesome, farm-fresh meat and eggs is cost-effective and relatively easy. Want to try? Here's how.

GETTING THE BEST EGGS

Getting the best eggs for your purposes means choosing the right breed for your purposes. You then must make sure you're providing the hens with the best possible diet and living conditions. You need to understand what factors affect egg laying and how to circumvent possible problems.

THE RIGHT HEN FOR THE JOB

Among production breeds, Leghorns are the queens of the henhouse; they lay early and often. Their compact, wiry bodies put everything they have into laying eggs. Yet they're not many small flock keepers' first choice. Leghorns are noisy and flighty, and if you eat your spent hens, there's not much stewed chicken on those bones when a Leghorn's laying days are through.

A slightly more substantial layer is the Red Star Sex Link hen, a reddish brown bird accented with flecks of white. The product of a Rhode Island Red rooster and a Leghorn hen, the Red Star Sex Link lays handsome brown eggs and is far less flaky than a Leghorn. Another benefit: since pullets are red and cockerels are white, you can tell hatchlings apart—hence the "Sex Link" part of her name.

Her close cousin is the gold-accented Black Star Sex Link hen (cockerels are black with white barring), whose mama was a Plymouth Rock and daddy a Rhode Island Red. The Black Star lays bigger eggs, though slightly fewer, than the Red Star. Like the Red Star, she's a fairly easygoing bird.

Old-time layers and dual-purpose chickens, such as Brahmas, Dominiques, Cochins, and Wyandottes, have a place in today's henhouse, too. They begin laying later and don't lay as many eggs, but they keep it up longer than production breed hens.

Bantams for eggs? Sure, why not? Bantam eggs are tiny—smaller than pee-wee eggs from the store! But fanciers claim they're the tastiest of all hens' eggs, and bantam layers require very little feed and space.

Though color is purely a matter of aesthetics, not taste, if you plan to sell extra eggs when you start your flock, choose a breed that lays the color most popular in your locale (see Pick a Color box). If you have fertile, organic, or free-range eggs, toot your horn! Consumers pay premium prices for these specialties and are tickled to have them. In most states, peddling eggs from your home doesn't require a business license, but it's best to be certain before tacking up a sign.

EGG-LAYING TIMETABLE

When your home-raised pullets are six weeks old and ready to leave the brooder, move them to their own safe haven, away from aggressive older

Research chicken breeds to select a hen who will lay eggs the color of your choice.

chickens. Switch their feed to a 15-16 percent protein grower ration and optional supplements like "big girl" scratch and greens. Don't forget to set out a free-choice grit container.

Around twenty weeks of age, upgrade to a 16-18 percent layer ration and add calcium-boosting, free-choice oyster shell alongside their grit. Never let feeders or waterers run dry. Keeping fresh, pure drinking water in front of your hens is a must! Even a few hours without water affect their lay. If your hens are super-layers, such as Black or Red Star Sex-Links, or from fast-maturing production Leghorn strains, they'll begin laying between twenty and twenty-four weeks of age.

A pullet's first eggs will be teensy treasures. New layers rarely grasp the concept of nest boxes, so you'll find eggs wherever they land. Tuck an artificial egg, such as a wooden or marble one, a sand-filled plastic Easter egg, or a golf ball, in each nest. Pretty soon your hens will understand and begin laying in the nesting boxes.

By week thirty-two, most hens will be up to form. They'll continue laying full bore for at least two years and can continue laying up to twelve years. As they age, hens' eggs will increase in size, but decrease in number.

Remember that hens don't lay while brooding or raising chickies, and they may stop laying as winter days grow short. Hens require fourteen hours of daylight to keep producing, so in northern climes lighting the henhouse is an absolute must. Add extra hours of light pre-sunrise so your chickens will naturally go to roost at dusk. Use a timer so you don't forget; it's important to be consistent. Just one or two days without additional lighting can throw production out of whack. Or give your hens a winter break; they'll ultimately last longer if you do.

Each year your girls will molt; they'll shed and regrow their feathers a few at a time. Molting generally begins as summer winds down and extends for twelve to eighteen weeks, through early fall. A fast molt is a fine chicken trait indeed because egg production slows or ceases as Ms. Hen molts. The sooner she's finished, the sooner she'll lay.

Pick a Color

Brown eggs
Aseel, Australorp, Sex Links (both Red and Black), Brahma, Buckeye, Chantecler, Cochin, Cornish, Delaware, Dominique, Faverolle, Java, Jersey Giant, Langshan, Malay, Marans, Naked Neck, New Hampshire, Orpington, Plymouth Rock, Rhode Island Red, Welsumer, Wyandotte

White eggs
Campine, Crevecoeur, Dorking, Houdan, La Fleche, Lamona, Leghorn, Minorca, Polish, Redcap, Buttercup, Silkie, Sultan, White Faced Black Spanish, Yokohama

Tinted eggs (not quite white)
Ancona, Campine, Catalina, Hamburg, Lakenvelder, Modern Game, Old English Game, Sumatra

Colored eggs
Araucana, Ameraucana, Easter Egger

Layer Requirements

Feed

Pullets, 6–20 weeks	15%–16% protein grower ration
Layers, 20 weeks and up	16%–18% protein layer ration
Breeders, 20 weeks and up	18% protein breeder or layer ration
Necessary supplements	Oyster shell for additional calcium; grit (not necessary if confined and eating commercial rations *only*)
Optional dietary supplements (using will upset the commercial feed's nutritional balance and may reduce egg production)	Scratch grains, greens, most garden produce, and fruit (no potato skins, no avocados), bugs, and other foraged goodies

Housing

Indoor floor space for free-range chickens and chickens with adequate outdoor runs and indoor roosts	Heavy breeds: 4 sq. ft. Light breeds: 3 sq. ft. Bantams: 2 sq. ft.
Outdoor run requirements for above	Heavy breeds: 10 sq. ft. Light breeds: 8 sq. ft. Bantams: 5 sq. ft.
Indoor floor space for confined birds without access to outdoor runs	Heavy breeds: 10 sq. ft. Light breeds: 8 sq. ft. Bantams: 5 sq. ft.
Starter Roosts (4 in. from floor and 12–14 in. between rails; move lower rail higher as birds mature)	Heavy breeds 6–20 weeks old: 6–8 in. of space; light breeds 4–18 weeks old: 4–6 in. of space; bantams 4–18 weeks old: 3–4 in. of space
Permanent Roosts	Heavy breeds: 10 in. of space, 18 in. from floor, and 16 in. between rails; Light breeds: 8 in. of space, 24 in. from floor, and 14 in. between rails; Bantams: 6 in. of space, 24 in. from floor, and 12 in. between rails
Nesting boxes	1 for every 4–5 hens; (1 for every 3 hens in flocks of 12 or less) Bed deeply; change litter every week
Feeders	1 standard hanging tube style feeder per 25 birds or 4 in. of trough space per hen
Waterers	1 inch waterer space per hen, providing at least 2 gal. of water per 25 birds
Lighting	One 25- to 40-watt bulb per 40 sq. ft. of floor space, placed at ceiling height above feeders/waterers; Provide 14–16 hours of light per day year-round

Stressed hens lay fewer eggs. A whole passel of things can stress chickens: extreme heat or cold, fright (don't let kids, pets, or predators harass them), illness, parasites, adding new chickens to the flock, or taking away familiar friends. Business as usual keeps stress down and is good for laying. Strive for peace and serenity in the henhouse if you love fresh eggs.

WHO'S BEEN EATING MY EGGS?

Everyone loves fresh eggs. Even hens. Egg eating begins innocently enough, when an egg is accidentally cracked or shattered and a curious hen takes a nibble. Mmm-mmm, good! She keeps her eyes peeled for more golden goodness and when she tucks in, her sisters' curiosity is piqued. They sample, too.

Yummy! One fine day, someone notices that if you peck really hard, you can sometimes serve yourself. Pretty soon, your flock is eating more eggs than you are.

What to do?

• Revamp your coop's nesting area. Provide more nests for the flock so there is less traffic, and ultimately fewer broken eggs. After all, it's a single broken egg that can trigger this hard-to-zap habit.

• Relocate nesting boxes away from the fast lane. Install them at least 24 inches from the floor in a secluded corner of the coop.

• Keep plenty of clean, cushiony litter in each box. Protective padding saves many an egg.

• Ban broodies from the henhouse.

Great-Tasting Eggs

Follow these tips for clean, great-tasting eggs:

• Use plenty of cushy nesting box litter and check it often. Remove muck promptly. Dump everything out and replace it with fresh, fluffy litter at least once a month.

• Collect eggs first thing in the morning and at least once or twice more during the day. The longer the eggs stay in the nests, the more likely they'll become mud-smeared, splotted upon, or cracked. For the same reason, supply plenty of nesting boxes. Cutting down on traffic really helps the eggs.

• Collect eggs in a natural fiber or coated wire basket (not the calf's drained nursing bucket or the horse's sweet feed scoop). To prevent breakage, don't stack them more than five layers deep.

• Don't clean eggs if they don't need it. Carefully chase minor spots with fine grit sandpaper. When you must wash soiled eggs, do it as soon as you can, before the eggs have cooled. Cooling causes shells to contract and suck dirt and bacteria into their pores.

• Use water that is 10 degrees warmer than the eggs themselves. This causes their contents to swell and shove surface dirt out and away from the shell pores. Gently scrub them in plain water or mild egg-cleaning detergent (available from poultry supply retailers). Never soak eggs, especially in cool water; water contaminates can be absorbed through the shells.

• Dry washed eggs before storing them.

• Refrigerate eggs in cartons, large end up. To preserve quality (and prevent development in fertile eggs), get them in the fridge as soon as you can. Date the cartons and rotate your stock, using up older cartons first.

• Eggs absorb odors from strongly scented foods like fish, garlic, onions, cantaloupe, and apples. Try not to store eggs with these items.

Egg yolks and crushed shells are tasty treats to a chicken. Promptly remove eggs from the hen-house or you may find that your birds eat more eggs than you do!

They're happier off by themselves and the nest they're setting in is one less for the rest of the hens to use, resulting in higher traffic in the remaining cubicles.

• Strive for stronger shells. Feed high-calcium commercial layer ration with oyster shell served up free choice.

• Pulverize egg shells you feed to your hens. They're a dandy source of calcium, and getting used to the taste won't give a hen that "Ah-ha!" moment when she realizes she's dining on egg.

Eggs for Sale!

In many places it's illegal to market farm eggs in another store or in a company's marked cartons, so carefully spritz pressed-paper egg cartons with cardboard box blockout before reusing them.

Otherwise, purchase generic cartons and advise customers to return them for refills, or ask them to bring their own containers when they come to buy your eggs.

• Stressed chickens pick. Keep everything in your hens' environment as low-key as you possibly can. Avoid changes in their daily routine and never let them run out of fresh feed and water. Don't introduce new chickens to an established laying flock, which triggers changes in social order. Keep them reasonably cool in July and warm in February. Absolutely avoid overcrowding and always handle laying hens in a quiet, compassionate manner.

• Don't push hens roughly out of nest boxes when collecting eggs. If a hen breaks eggs as she hastily retreats, clean up the mess right away.

• Identify culprits and cull them to pet homes—or even the stew pot. You'll know them by the dried yolk remnants decorating their beaks and heads.

• Don't assume your hens are noshing all those eggs. Predators such as skunks, opossums, and the occasional snake fancy chicken eggs, too.

This light Brahma leaves the row of open-topped nesting boxes, leaving a fresh-laid egg for our breakfast.

TASTY CHICKEN

If you want to grow a lot of tasty chickens in a short time, start with meat-breed chicks. Chicken-raising newbies who spring for low-priced Leghorn cockerels will be disappointed. Bred for laying eggs, not for making meat, light breed chickens guzzle twice the feed and never flesh out to prime eating size.

SUPER OR DUAL-PURPOSE BIRDS

Super-broilers convert feed to flesh at lightning speed. They take eight to twelve weeks from hatch to slaughter at 4 to 5 pounds live weight, or they can be slaughtered earlier (at five to six weeks as Cornish Game Hens) or later (at twelve to twenty weeks and 6 to 8 pounds live weight) if the raiser prefers birds of a different size.

Old-fashioned dual-purpose breed chickens make delicious eating, too, although they mature slower and demand more feed for each pound of weight they pack onto their sturdy frames. Old standbys like Rhode Island Reds, White Rocks, and New

No Names Please

Years ago, we raised chickens for meat. Just one batch, as it turned out. Our mistake: we ignored the age-old adage—don't give your food names. We made pets out of our boisterous young cockerels and when processing day rolled around, we could only bring ourselves to kill a few. We gave the rest away, and two weeks later, we were vegetarians. Sage advice from she who knows: don't give your broiler chicks names!

Hampshires need twelve to sixteen weeks to grow to broiler size but their slower-growing ways spare them the health and structural problems that super-broilers experience during their far shorter lives. Some say old-fashioned breeds are more flavorful, too.

Most super-broilers and popular dual-purpose breeds are yellow-skinned, white-feathered chickens, simply because that's the kind of bird Americans prefer. Brown and black semi-super-broilers can be ordered from large hatcheries like Stromberg's and McMurray's. They're more active than white Cornish-Rocks and they bloom a smidge more slowly, but like dual-purpose breed broilers, they're less susceptible to the structural problems that plague their faster maturing kin.

BROILER'S TIMETABLE AND REQUIREMENTS

Whichever type you prefer, you must feed your meat peeps 20-22 percent protein broiler starter. Lower protein products simply won't do. Check with your feed store before chicks arrive since they may not keep broiler feeds in stock. Figure one hundred pounds of starter per twenty-five chicks.

Dual-purpose breeds such as this silver-laced Wyandotte rooster produce good meat, but mature more slowly than super-broilers such as Cornish game hens.

Adding vitamin and electrolyte powdered supplement to your new chicks' waterer at the manufacturer's dosage recommendation can help prevent leg weakness in certain broiler breeds.

When your chicks leave the brooder at roughly six weeks old, switch to broiler finisher (regular—not broiler; 18-20 percent chick starter will do). They'll remain on this ration until they're slaughtered.

Most folks raise broilers indoors, allowing 2 square feet of floor space between 6 and 10 weeks of age, then 3 square feet until slaughter. Continuous, ultra-low lighting encourages nighttime noshing, which is especially important during sizzling summer climates. Some raisers limit feed intake, others keep feed in front of their birds all the time.

Broilers—Roasters

Broiler / Roaster Requirements

Feeding

Broiler chicks, first 6 weeks	20%-22% protein broiler starter ration
Broilers, 6 weeks to slaughter	18%-20% broiler finishing ration
Necessary supplements	Grit (not necessary if confined and eating commercial rations *only*)
Optional dietary supplements (feeding will upset commercial feeds' nutritional balance and birds will mature more slowly)	Scratch grains, greens, most garden produce and fruit (no potato skins, no avocados), bugs and other foraged goodies
Optional drink water additives	Vitamin-electrolyte supplement

Housing

Indoor floor space	6 to 10 weeks of age: 2 sq. ft.; 10 weeks to slaughter: 3 sq. ft.
Roosts	None
Feeders	1 standard hanging tube style feeder per 20 birds or 4 in. of trough space per bird
Waterers	1 in. of waterer space per bird, providing at least 2 gal. of water per 25 birds

Whichever method you choose, make sure that plenty of clean, cool water is available. Adding a vitamin-electrolyte product to their drinking water is a wise idea, too.

BROILER DON'TS

Unfortunately, astronomical weight gain comes at a hefty price. Cornish-Rock broilers' broad-chested, meaty bodies mature faster than their skeletal structures can support them. Crippled legs and crooked breastbones are the norm.

Lame birds crouch to ease pain and develop breast blisters. Super-broilers are also prone to heart attacks. For best results with swift-maturing meat birds, heed these ploys:

- Stir litter often; keep it fluffy and dry. Crouching on hard-packed litter irritates broilers' keel bones. It's a major cause of breast blisters.

- Don't give meat chickens roosts; as they hop to the floor after roosting, they'll damage their legs. Pressing against these hard objects causes breast blisters, too. Remove anything in their environment they could leap up on: rocks, boards, doors, ledges, protrusions of any sort.

- Don't capture or carry meat fowl by their legs.

- Don't startle or chase these injury-prone fowl. Keep surprises down to a minimum. Broiler stampedes equal

This barnyard rooster is mostly Old English Game, a good forager and, therefore, good in free-range situations.

torn muscles, slipped joints, and heart attacks.

• Remove lame chickens from the flock. Lodge them in separate quarters with easy access to food and water. Many will recover within a week. To prevent needless suffering, cull any birds who don't.

MAKING MEAT DOWN ON THE FARM

Butcher broiler chickens at the same time. Or, create a continuous home supply by starting a new brood when the first is four weeks old, then slaughtering one-fourth of the older group at intervals of seven, eight, nine, and ten weeks of age. Process roasters at 6 to 8 pounds live weight. Don't carry them much beyond that. The older they get, the less efficiently they convert feed to meat.

If you've never processed chickens before, have someone show you how. The process isn't tricky, but it should be done with precision. Second best, print or download a heavily illustrated university publication and follow their instructions to the letter.

Keep it Clean

To quash disease and avert parasite problems, always strip, scrub, and thoroughly disinfect your broiler quarters between batches of birds.

If you do, and you raise your chickens indoors, you usually needn't vaccinate or deworm them, especially if you feed medicated commercial rations.

Albumen—egg white

Alektorophobia—(also spelled Alektrophobia) the fear of chickens

American Bantam Association (ABA)—an organization devoted to the standardization and promotion of bantam chickens and ducks

American Poultry Association (APA)—an organization devoted to the standardization and promotion of large size chickens and ducks

Avian—having to do with birds; avian medicine, avian art, etc.

Bantam—a miniature chicken weighing 1 to 3 pounds and 1/4 to 1/5 the size of large breed chickens; some are scaleddown versions of large breeds but a few bantam breeds have no full-size counterparts; slang: banty (plural: banties)

Barny—a mixed-breed chicken; also called a barnyard chicken or, if bantam size, a barnyard banty

Beak—the protruding mouth parts of a bird

Beard—the tuft of feathers under the beaks of muffed breeds such as the Ameraucana, Belgian d'Uccle, and Houdan

Bedding—the thick layer of cushiony, absorbent material used to line nest boxes and poultry building floors; also called litter

Billing out—the act of chickens using their beaks to scoop feed out of a feeder and onto the floor; filling feeders only-partly discourages this wasteful habit

Bleaching—the fading of color from a aging, yellow-skinned laying hen's beak, shanks, and vent

Bloom—the protective coating on an unwashed egg

Blowout—vent damage caused by laying a huge egg

Booted—having feathers on shanks and toes

Breaking up—the act of convincing a broody hen that she doesn't want to set

Breed—a group of birds or animals having approximately the same background, body shape, and features;

breeds "breed true" when an offspring from two individuals of the same breed resemble her parents

Breeders—birds from which fertile eggs are collected for artificial incubation purposes

Broiler—a tender 9- to 12-week-old meat chicken generally weighing 2.5–3.5 pounds; also called a fryer

Brood—(verb) to keep chicks warm inside a heated enclosure called a brooder or brooder box, or under a hen; (noun) the young of a chicken

Broody hen—one who, through hormonal changes, stops laying and elects to hatch eggs or care for baby chicks; also called a broody

Candle—to evaluate the contents of an egg by holding it up to a strong light source

Candler—the strong light source used to candle eggs

Cannibalism—the habit stressed chickens have of pecking other chickens or themselves until they draw blood; a bloodied chicken often is killed by her peers

Cape—the narrow feathers between a chicken's neck and back

Capon—a castrated male chicken

Cecum—a pouch-like internal organ located where small and large intestines connect

Chalazae—the white, stringy cords on opposite ends of an egg yolk that center it within the egg

Chook—originally Australian slang; a common synonym for chicken

Class—a group of chickens developed in a certain locale (e.g., American, Asiatic, Continental classes)

Clean-legged—having no feathers on the shanks

Cloaca—the chamber inside a chicken's vent where her digestive, excretory, and reproductive tracts meet

Clutch—a batch of eggs hatched in an incubator or under a hen; all the eggs laid by a hen on consecutive days before she skips a day to begin a new laying cycle

Coccidiostat—a drug used to prevent the common protozoal infection, coccideosis; often added to commercial chick starter rations

Cock—a one-year-old or older male chicken; also called a rooster

Cockerel—a male chicken less than one year old

Comb—the fleshy, red appendage atop a chicken's head

Conformation—an animal or bird's body structure

Coop—a building where chickens reside

Crest—the wild topknot of feathers adorning the heads of crested breeds such as Polish, Crevecoeur, Houdon, and Silkie chickens; also called a topknot

Crop—the expandable pouch of tissue in a chicken's lower esophagus where food is temporarily stored before digestion begins

Crossbred—a chicken with parents of two different breeds

Cull—to eliminate a bird from the flock

Debeak—to burn or snip off the tip of a chicken's upper beak to prevent cannibalism

Dual-purpose breed—one who doesn't lay as many eggs as laying breeds nor mature as fast or as large as hybrid meat breeds but who lays more eggs than meat breeds and makes more meat than layers; an all-rounder

Dub—to trim a rooster's comb and snip off his wattles. Sometimes done to prevent frostbite or remove frostbitten tissue; Old English Game cocks must be dubbed in order to be shown

Dust bathing—the act of a chicken wallowing in dirt to clean its feathers and discourage external parasites

Earlobes—the patches of fleshy, bare skin below a chicken's external auditory meatuses

Egg tooth—a minuscule, sharp projection on a hatching chick's beak used to peck holes in her shell

Embryo—an unhatched, developing chick

Embryology—a branch of science devoted to the study of embryonic development

Exhibition breeds—fancy chickens raised for show instead of production

Feather-legged—having feathered shanks

Fertility—the state of being fertile

Finish—the amount of fat beneath the skin of a broiler or roaster chicken

Free-range chickens—uncaged fowl allowed to forage wherever they choose

Frizzle—feathers that curl instead of laying flat; also a specific breed of chicken having frizzled feathers

Fryer—a tender nine- to twelve-week-old meat chicken generally weighing 2.5–3.5 pounds; also called a broiler

Gallus domesticus—the domestic chicken

Gallus gallus—the Red Jungle Fowl, also called Gallus bankiva

Genus—a group of closely related animals or birds that differ very slightly from one another (as *Gallus gallus* from *Gallus domesticus*)

Gizzard—the tough internal organ where food is macerated

Grade—to sort according to quality

Grit—pebbles, sand, or a commercial "grit" product ingested by a chicken and used by the gizzard to grind food

Hackles—a rooster's neck feathers; sometimes collectively called his cape

Hatch—a group of chicks who emerge from their shells at about the same time

Hatchability—the state of being capable of hatching

Hen—a female chicken at least one year old

Hen-feathered rooster—a male chicken having rounded (not pointed) sex feathers

Humidity—the amount of moisture in the air

Hybrid—a crossbred bird or animal bred for a certain looks, traits, or behaviors; when bred together, hybrids don't produce offspring with their own characteristics

Inbred chicken—the offspring of closely related parents; inbreeding is a valuable tool by which breeders set certain characteristics within their chosen bloodlines

Incubation—the act of hatching eggs

Keel—a chicken's breastbone

Large chicken, large fowl—the original, "normal-sized" chicken (as opposed to bantams), sometimes erroneously called standard chickens

Layer, laying hen—a chicken kept for egg production

Litter—the thick layer of cushiony, absorbent material used to line laying nests and poultry building floors; also called bedding

Mate—to pair a male and female animal or bird for breeding purposes

Meat breed chicken—one developed for quick growth and heavy muscling

Molt—the annual shedding and renewal of plumage

Muff—a grouping of feathers bristling out from the sides of bearded breeds' faces; also called whiskers

Nest—a dark, secluded place where a hen feels it's safe to lay her eggs

Nesting box—man-made cubicles placed in hen houses so hens can lay their eggs away from the main flow of traffic

Nest egg—an artificial egg placed in a nest to encourage hens to lay there

Nest run—ungraded eggs

Oviduct—the tube-like internal organ of female birds through which a passing egg is encased in albumen, shell membranes, and shell

Pasty butt—diarrhea stuck to a chick or older chicken's vent area

Pecking order—the social order of chickens

Perch—(noun) the place, usually elevated rails, where chickens sleep at night; also called a roost; (verb) the act of resting on a roost

Pick out—vent damage caused by other chickens' pecking

Pin bones—pubic bones; two sharp, skinny bones ending near the vent

Pinfeathers—the tips of newly emerging feathers

Plumage—feathers

Pip—(verb) the act of an emerging chick breaking a hole in her shell as part of the hatching process; (noun) the hole a hatching chick makes

Pullet—a female chicken less than one year of age

Purebred—a chicken whose parents are both the same breed

Roaster—a three- to five-month-old meat chicken of either sex weighing 4–6 pounds

Roost—(noun) the place, usually elevated rails, where chickens sleep at night, also called a perch; (verb) the act of perching

Rooster—a male chicken at least one year of age; also called a cock

Saddle—collectively, the feathers on a rooster's back, just before the tail

Scratch—(verb) the act of scratching the ground in search of food; (noun) any grain product fed to chickens

Set—the act of allowing or encouraging a broody hen to incubate eggs

Sex-link breeds—breeds in which male and female chicks hatch in different colors or patterns, thus making accurate sexing immediately possible

Sexed chicks—all cockerels or all pullets separated by sex

Sex feathers—rounded hackle, saddle, and tail feathers on a hen; pointed hackle, saddle, and tail feathers on a rooster

Shank—the lower part of a chicken's leg between its claw and first joint

Sickle feather—a long, curved rooster tail feather

Shell membranes—two thin membranes immediately inside of an egg shell

Spent hen—a worn-out hen no longer laying well

Spurs—the sharp pointed appendages on a rooster's shanks

Standard—a description in word and picture of a breed's ideal specimen

Started pullets—sixteen- to twenty-two-week-old pullets on the brink of laying; usually purchased from a specialist breeder

Starter—commercial feed ration formulated for newly hatched chicks; there are two formulations, regular and broiler chick starters

Starve out—the act of newly hatched chicks refusing to eat

Stewing hen—a tough, old hen suitable only for pressurized or moist, slow cooking

Straight run—newly hatched unsexed chicks; a package of straight run chicks contains both cockerels and pullets

Strain—a group of animals or birds within a breed or variety, developed by a single breeder or small group of breeders; animals or birds of the same strain are very uniform and usually share common bloodlines

Stub—down on the legs of a supposedly clean-legged chicken

Tin hen—(slang) an artificial incubator

Trio—a rooster and two hens of the same breed and variety

Type—a breed's look; the distinctive size, shape, and appearance that indicate what breed a chicken belongs to

Vent—the cloaca's outside opening, through which a chicken eliminates and lays eggs

Wattles—two dangles of red flesh drooping down from the outer edges of a chicken's chin

Resources

HATCHERIES

BELT HATCHERY (CALIFORNIA)
http://www.belthatchery.com
(559) 264-2090
Belt Hatchery offers the usual commercial and backyard breeds and a small selection of fancies.

BLACK FOREST HATCHERY (KENTUCKY)
http://www.blackforestpoultry.com
(859) 294-7484
mmeers@qx.net
Black Forest Hatchery specializes in fancy and rare breed bantam chicks and hatching eggs, but they sell commercial and fancy chicks, too. Their site is especially information-rich; the Predators and Egg Candling pages are especially useful. The Black Forest Hatchery brochure is downloadable in PDF format.

CACKLE HATCHERY (MISSOURI)
http://www.cacklehatchery.com
(417)-532-4581
cacklehatchery@cacklehatchery.com
Cackle Hatchery sells a huge array of fancy, heirloom, and commercial day-old chicks. Their specialty is Old English Game varieties—dozens—and all are pictured on their colorful Web site. Cackle Hatchery's brochure is free, or order their lavishly illustrated color catalog for $3.

C. M. ESTES HATCHERY, INC. (MISSOURI)
http://www.esteshatchery.com
(417) 862-3593
Estes Hatchery markets a selection of commercial and fancy day-old chicks, including bantam fancies. Their Web site features pictures and descriptions of the breeds they sell.

HOFFMAN HATCHERY, INC. (PENNSYLVANIA)
http://www.hoffmanhatchery.com
Hoffman Hatchery carries commercial

and fancy breed chicks, books, and a selection of poultry needs and equipment. Their print catalog is free.

McKinney Poultry (Missouri)
http://www.mckinneypoultry.com/
(573) 518-0535
gdmckinn@i1.net
McKinney Poultry sells many breeds and varieties of exhibition-grade chicks. Download their price list or request a free print copy.

Murray McMurray Hatchery (Iowa)
http://www.mcmurrayhatchery.com
(800) 456-3280
Chicks of every conceivable breed and size, hatching eggs, equipment, feed (including their own organic mix) and supplements, books and videos, even t-shirts and Amish egg baskets—if it has anything to do with chickens, it's in Murray McMurray's free catalog.

Privett Hatchery (New Mexico)
http://www.privetthatchery.com
(877) PRIVETT
privetth@yahoo.com
Privett Hatchery offers a fine selection of commercial, fancy, and rare breed chicks, including bantams.

Sand Hill Preservation Center (Iowa)
http://www.sandhillpreservation.com/
Poultry.html
(563) 246-2299
sandhill@fbcom.net
Sand Hill Preservation Center is dedicated to the preservation of more than one thousand varieties of heirloom vegetables, flowers, fruits, grains and poultry. They sell many rare and heritage breeds (and a selection of more common ones) via their online and (free) print catalogs.

Stromberg's Chicks & Gamebirds Unlimited (Minnesota)
http://www.strombergschickens.com
(218) 587-2222
info@strombergschickens.com
Stromberg's offers a staggering variety of live poultry and hatching eggs, supplies, books, and videos. You can even buy mature chickens from Stromberg's lavish fifty-page color catalog—ask for it, it's free!

Welp Hatchery (Iowa)
http://www.welphatchery.com
(800) 458-4473
bkollasch@welphatchery.com
Welp Hatchery sells a wide variety of commercial, fancy, and rare breed day-old chicks along with the equipment and supplies you'll need to raise them. Download their price list in PDF form or request a free Welp Hatchery brochure.

Penn State Poultry Extension's Hatcheries on the Web (Pennsylvania)
http://ulisse.cas.psu.edu/ext/Hatcheries
.html
Locate a hatchery in your area by visiting the Penn State Poultry Extension's Web page.

RANCH & LIVESTOCK LINKS— HATCHERIES

http://ranchlinks.com/Livestock/ Poultry/Hatcheries

Ranch & Livestock Links directs surfers to the best of the agricultural Web, from livestock associations to government agencies to chickens (almost seven thousand links in all). Their hatchery pages lead to several dozen hatcheries, the better to find one in your locale.

ORGANIZATIONS

AMERICAN BANTAM ASSOCIATION/ABA

http://www.bantamclub.com
(973) 383-6944

Founded in 1914, the American Bantam Association promotes the breeding, exhibition, and selling of purebred bantam chickens and ducks. Visit its Web site to join the ABA, access breed club and member links, purchase books and other merchandise and read about the organization's many programs.

AMERICAN LIVESTOCK BREEDS CONSERVANCY/ALBC

http://www.albc-usa.org
(919) 542-5704
albc@albc-usa.org

The American Livestock Breeds Conservancy works to protect nearly one hundred breeds of cattle, goats, horses, asses, sheep, swine, and poultry from extinction. Visit the site to learn how you can help.

AMERICAN PASTURED POULTRY PRODUCERS ASSOCIATION/APPPA

http://apppa.org
(715) 667-5501
grit@apppa.org

The APPPA unites pastured poultry producers and distributes pastured poultry resources to consumers and potential producers. Visit their site to read archived articles, download the APPPA brochure or locate a pastured poultry producer in your locale.

AMERICAN POULTRY ASSOCIATION/APA

http://www.ampltya.com
(508) 473-8769

Founded in February of 1873, the American Poultry Association sanctions poultry shows and publishes the APA Standard of Perfection (the rules by which purebred poultry is shown), a yearbook, and a quarterly newsletter. Use the pull-down menus at the APA site to access a treasure trove of avian information; their Health Series and "Raising Birds in the City" (find it in the Useful Information menu) are especially well written.

NEW ENGLAND HERITAGE BREEDS CONSERVANCY/NEHBC

http://www.nehbc.org
(413) 443-8356
contact@NEHBC.org

The Heritage Breeds Conservancy works to preserve historic and endangered breeds of poultry and livestock. Conservators from across the United States and Canada are listed in the NEHBC Breeder's Directory and participate in the online forum and marketplace listings. A nice selection of conservation-related links rounds out this informative Web site.

NATIONAL CENTER FOR APPROPRIATE TECHNOLOGY/NCAT
http://www.sustainablepoultry.ncat.org
(800) 346-9140
For the past twenty-five years, the National Center for Appropriate Technology has served economically disadvantaged people by providing information and access to appropriate technologies that can help improve their lives. The ATTRA Project, funded by the U.S. Department of Agriculture, is managed by NCAT. ATTRA provides information and other technical assistance to farmers, ranchers, extension agents, educators, and others involved in sustainable agriculture throughout the United States. Visit NCAT/ATTRA's Sustainable Poultry Web site to view or download dozens of valuable ATTRA bulletins, or phone to request a free information packet tailored specifically for you.

THE NATIONAL POULTRY IMPROVEMENT PLAN/NPIP
http://www.aphis.usda.gov/vs/npip
The USDA certifies breeders and hatcheries, ensuring that their chickens (and other poultry) test free of the deadly Pullorum Disease. Read about the National Poultry Improvement Plan, locate participating hatcheries via the NPIP online directory, and request a copy of the free booklet, "Helping You, the Poultry Breeder," and their free video on preventing Pullorum.

THE POULTRY CLUB OF GREAT BRITAIN/PCGB
http://www.poultryclub.org
Founded in 1877, the Poultry Club of Great Britain declares itself the world's biggest poultry club. Don't miss this information-rich site! Visit all of the items listed in the menu—you won't be disappointed when you do.

RARE BREEDS SURVIVAL TRUST/RBST
http://www.rbst.org.uk
The Rare Breeds Survival Trust (the United Kingdom's equivalent of the American Livestock Breeds Conservancy) currently monitors seventy-three breeds of rare poultry and livestock, including many concurrently tracked in North America by the ALBC.

SOCIETY FOR THE PRESERVATION OF POULTRY ANTIQUITIES/SPPA
http://www.feathersite.com/Poultry/
SPPA/SPPA.html
Fascinated by heirloom chickens? Join the SPPA and help preserve and promote them. The group promotes rare breeds of chickens, ducks, geese, and turkeys and sponsors awards, shows, and exhibitions.

CHICKEN SUPPLIES
Most of the businesses listed under Hatcheries also sell a wide variety of poultry keeping needs.

CHICKEN DIAPERS
http://www.browneggblueegg.com/
BirdDiaper.html
r_in_ar@yahoo.com

Ruth Cahill custom-fabricates stretchy fabric chicken diapers in fourteen cool colors (including camo).

EGGANIC INDUSTRIES

http://www.henspa.com
(800) 783-6344
wskeel@gamewood.net

Egganic Industries manufactures neat, prefabricated chicken coops on wheels. When touring the Egganic Industries Web site, click on Fun Facts to access their collection of great chicken resources.

EGGCARTONS.COM

http://www.eggcartons.com
(888) 852-5340

If you sell eggs, visit this site to order plain or imprinted paper, foam, and plastic egg cartons at discount prices. Also available are incubators, feeders, waterers, books, and a fine selection of chicken-themed gifts. Little Giant incubator-owners take note: free Little Giant product manuals are downloadable from this site!

KEMP'S KOOPS

http://www.poultrysupply.com

Kemp's Koops sells poultry, chicken, gamebird, and exotic avian supplies and incubators for hatching fertile eggs.

NASCO FARM & RANCH SUPPLIES

http://www.eNASCO.com
(800) 558-9595
info@eNASCO.com

Nasco boasts the largest farm catalog in the world, and it's free. Nasco carries a wide selection of poultry supplies, including less standard items like portable chicken coops that house up to twenty-five hens and a PVC Pastured Poultry hoop pen.

POULTRYMAN'S SUPPLY COMPANY

http://www.poultrymansupply.com
(859) 745-4944
info@poultrymansupply.com

Poultryman's Supply offers incubators, brooders, waterers and feeders, medications, books, leg bands, egg cartons, and more. Prices include postage.

SMITH POULTRY & GAME BIRD SUPPLY

http://www.poultrysupplies.com
(913) 879-2587
Smith@poultrysupplies.com

Smith Poultry and Game Bird Supply sells incubation supplies, brooders, nest boxes, netting, legbands, waterers, feeders, medications, vaccines, vitamins, disinfectants, books, and a lot of other products that chicken raisers of all sorts will appreciate. Their print catalog is free.

UNIVERSITY RESOURCES

Major state universities and all state extension services distribute papers and bulletins of interest to chicken owners. Compile an up-to-date free library of chicken materials by downloading PDF files and bulletins and binding the printouts to create your own personal "everything about chickens" reference book.

University of Arkansas Extension

http://www.uaex.edu

Access University of Arkansas' "Fun With Incubation" bulletin by clicking on Agriculture, then Poultry, then Fun With Incubation. Read it online, download it in PDF format, or order a print copy (it's free). Click on Small Flock Information on the Poultry page to access dozens of university publications.

University of California Poultry Web Page

http://animalscience.ucdavis.edu/Avian/pubs.htm

Download scores of University of California/Davis poultry fact sheets, leaflets, booklets, and technical papers in free PDF format. Check out "Common Incubation Problems: Causes and Remedies," "Egg-Type Layer Flock Care Practices," "Broiler Care Practices," and "Starting and Managing Small Poultry Units."

Clemson University Extension

http://hgic.clemson.edu

Download a great egg incubating bulletin compliments of Clemson University. Click on Extension Home, then Publications (at the top of the page), then Digital Publications Only. Next, click on Animal and Veterinary Sciences, then Poultry. There it is!

Florida Cooperative Extension's Electronic Data Information Source

http://edis.ifas.ufl.edu

To access the University of Florida's many chicken publications, click on Topic Areas, then Topic Index, then C (for chicken) and P (for poultry). "Common Poultry Diseases," "Internal Parasites in Backyard Chicken Flocks," and "Vaccination of Small Poultry Flocks" are a few noteworthy titles.

University of Georgia College of Agricultural and Environmental Sciences Cooperative Extension Service

http://extension.caes.uga.edu

The University of Georgia College of Agricultural and Environmental Sciences publishes thousands of online and PDF format documents. To locate chicken titles click on Publications, then Subject Listing, and scroll down to Poultry Science near the bottom of the list. "Management Guide for the Backyard Flock" and "Nutrition for the Backyard Flock" are especially useful publications.

University of Illinois Extension Incubation and Embryology

www.urbanext.uiuc.edu/eggs/index.html

Written for upper elementary to high school students and their teachers, this material covers everything from History of Breeds and Chicken Feet to Constructing an Egg Candler and Incubation Troubleshooting.

Kansas State Research and Extension /Kansas State Center for Sustainable Agriculture and Alternative Crops

http://www.oznet.ksu.edu

Click on Publications, then Livestock, then Poultry to access Kansas State University's outstanding chicken bulletins. This site offers a slew of great titles including "Processing Farm Raised Poultry," "Guide in Selecting and Preparing Poultry for Exhibition," and "Cannibalism in the Small Poultry Flock." Also collect a plethora of vintage bulletins now in PDF format by clicking on Historic Publications on the home page. Dozens of chicken publications are listed under Bulletins 1888–Current and Circulars 1910–1949.

UNIVERSITY OF KENTUCKY COLLEGE OF AGRICULTURE

http://www.ca.uky.edu/agripedia
To access an array of useful University of Kentucky Agripedia Web pages, charts, and bulletins, click Subject Index, then click C (for chicken) and P (for poultry).

UNIVERSITY OF MAINE COOPERATIVE EXTENSION

http://www.umext.maine.edu
The University of Maine Cooperative Extension offers several useful chicken bulletins downloadable in PDF format. To reach them click on Publications, then Online Catalog, then Home, Gardening, and Backyard or Agriculture—Dairy, Livestock and Poultry. "Hatching Your Own Chicks," "Match Your Need to the Right Breed," and "Biological Control of Coccidiosis in Small Poultry Flocks" are especially useful.

MARYLAND COOPERATIVE EXTENSION

http://www.agnr.umd.edu/MCE/index.cfm
Click on Publications, then Crops, Livestock & Nursery, then scroll down through the list to access University of Maryland poultry bulletins. Don't miss "Homemade Comfort Cages for Small Poultry Flocks," "Raising Your Home Chicken Flock," and "Good Neighbors; A Health Program for Small and Specialty Flocks."

MICHIGAN STATE UNIVERSITY EXTENSION

http://www.msue.msu.edu/home
To access Michigan State University Extension's chicken bulletins, click on Information Resources, then Information Access Center, then Animals, then Poultry.

UNIVERSITY OF MINNESOTA EXTENSION SERVICE

http://www.extension.umn.edu
Peruse or download a slew of University of Minnesota chicken materials by clicking Farm, then Poultry in the left hand menus. Their "Home Processing of Poultry" bulletin is outstanding.

MISSISSIPPI STATE UNIVERSITY EXTENSION SERVICE

http://msucares.com
Finding chicken resources at the MSU Cares site is the essence of simplicity. Click on Poultry in the menu and there you are!

UNIVERSITY OF MISSOURI EXTENSION

http://muextension.missouri.edu
University of Missouri Extension offers

an impressive selection of useful chicken bulletins. Access them by clicking Publications, then Agriculture, then Poultry. Best choices include "Incubation of Poultry," "Managing a Family Chicken Flock," and "Brooding and Growing Chicks."

UNIVERSITY OF NEBRASKA-LINCOLN INSTITUTE OF AGRICULTURE AND NATURAL RESOURCES
http://ianrpubs.unl.edu
Don't miss the collection of great chicken bulletins available (online and in print) via the University of Nebraska-Lincoln Institute of Agriculture and Natural Resources Web site. Reach them by clicking on Poultry under Browse Publications. Don't miss the Home Flock series and "Cannibalism; Cause and Prevention in Poultry."

UNIVERSITY OF NEBRASKA COOPERATIVE EXTENSION IN LANCASTER COUNTY, 4H EMBRYOLOGY PROGRAM
http://lancaster.unl.edu/4h/Embryology/
This educational site provides heaps of information suitable for the classroom or fun learning at home. Material includes video and wonderful photos on topics such as candling and hatching.

NORTH CAROLINA COOPERATIVE EXTENSION
http://www.ces.ncsu.edu
Click on Agriculture and Food, then Animal Agriculture, then Poultry, then Technical Information to access North Carolina State University's fine chicken publications.

NORTH DAKOTA STATE UNIVERSITY EXTENSION SERVICE
http://www.ag.ndsu.nodak.edu/abeng/plans/POULTRY.htm
Find oodles of free, downloadable poultry housing and equipment plans at North Dakota State University's Extension Ag & Biosystems Engineering Web site.

OHIO STATE UNIVERSITY EXTENSION
http://extension.osu.edu
Click on Crops & Livestock, then Poultry to access Ohio State University chicken bulletins. Outstanding publications include "Poultry Pest Management," "Preventive Medicine for Backyard Chickens," and "Incubation and Embryonic Development."

OKLAHOMA STATE UNIVERSITY AGRICULTURAL COMMUNICATIONS SERVICES
http://osuextra.okstate.edu
Click on Animals, then Poultry to access Oklahoma State University's excellent PDF bulletins. Don't miss "Predators; Thieves in the Night," "Home Processing of Poultry," and "Poultry for the Small Producer."

OREGON STATE UNIVERSITY EXTENSION
http://eesc.orst.edu
To access Oregon State University's chicken bulletins, scroll down the home page to Agriculture and click on More. Then under Publication Topics, click on Poultry & Rabbits. Don't miss "Hatching Small Numbers of Eggs," "Why Did My Chickens Stop Laying," and "Brooding & Rearing Baby Chicks."

PENN STATE EXTENSION & OUTREACH
http://www.extension.psu.edu
Don't miss this site. Penn State's chicken resource pages are truly outstanding. To reach them, click on Agriculture, then Poultry, then choose your topics of interest.

ANIMAL EXTENSION SERVICES AT PURDUE UNIVERSITY
http://ag.ansc.purdue.edu/anscext
Some of the Internet's most comprehensive chicken resources pages are accessible through the Animal Extension Services at Purdue University Web page. Click on Species Info, then Poultry Page, then Publications.

UNIVERSITY OF TENNESSEE EXTENSION
http://www.utextension.utk.edu
To navigate to chicken bulletins offered by the University of Tennessee Extension, click on Publications, then Animals Livestock, then Poultry.

TEXAS A&M UNIVERSITY POULTRY SCIENCE DEPARTMENT
http://gallus.tamu.edu
Click on Extension Publications in the pull-down Extension Service menu to access dozens of chicken management, chicken meat, and egg bulletins including "The Home Broiler Flock," "Nutrition and Feeding of Show Poultry," and "Curing and Smoking Poultry."

VIRGINIA COOPERATIVE EXTENSION
http://www.ext.vt.edu
To reach Virginia Cooperative Extension's outstanding chicken bulletin offerings, click on Educational Programs & Resources, then Livestock, Poultry & Dairy, then Poultry, then Small Specialty Flock. To access additional small flock publications, click on Management Requirements and Troubleshooting.

WEST VIRGINIA UNIVERSITY EXTENSION SERVICE
http://www.wvu.edu
Peruse West Virginia University's exceptional chicken resources, by clicking Agriculture, then Poultry. From the Poultry page, visit any of several great links pages or click Poultry Online Resources to download West Virginia University bulletins, including an exceptionally fine selection of small flock publications.

UNIVERSITY OF WISCONSIN EXTENSION
http://cecommerce.uwex.edu
The University of Wisconsin offers only one chicken bulletin but it's a honey: an eighteen-page 4-H manual titled "Bantams," free as a PDF download. To find it, click on Agriculture, then Livestock and Poultry, then scroll down to Poultry. An inexpensive print version is available for purchase.

OTHER USEFUL WEB SITES
AMERICAN HOLISTIC VETERINARY MEDICINE ASSOCIATION/AHVMA
http://ahvma.org
Visit the American Holistic Veterinary Medicine Association Web site to locate a holistic vet for your chickens.

Association of Avian Veterinarians/AAV

http://www.aav.org

When your sick or injured chicken needs specialist, find one via the Association of Avian Veterinarians Web site.

Backyard Chickens

http://www.backyardchickens.com

Backyard Chickens is a large, comprehensive site incorporating a Message Board with more than 4,600 registered users, a Learning Center, an Image Gallery, Fun Pages, and a well-stocked online store. Building a backyard coop or a chicken tractor? Learn how to do it here. The Breeds feature at this site is especially well done.

Bird-Click

http://www.geocities.com/birdtrain

If you'd like to clicker train your chicken and teach her to do tricks, walk on a leash, or sing when you ask her, visit Bird-Click to learn how.

Brown Egg, Blue Egg

http://www.browneggblueegg.com

Brown Egg, Blue Egg belongs to Alan Stanford, PhD, whose tips appear in this book. View his Bearded Silkies and bantam Araucanas (he sells chicks and adult birds) or peruse the wealth of chicken information linked from his pages. If you love chickens or want to know how they work as pets, click on Stories. The Articles link takes you to scores of fascinating articles. Brown Egg, Blue Egg is a two-thumbs-up site.

Chicken Breeds

http://www.ansi.okstate.edu/poultry/chickens

The Department of Animal Science at Oklahoma State University's chicken breeds Web site pictures and describes more than eighty chicken breeds. It's a honey!

Chicken Feed: The World of Chickens

http://www.lionsgrip.com/chickens.html

The Chicken Feed Web site brings you: "Sources of natural chicken feed, knowledge about traditional ways of feeding chickens around the world and in old times, and health before profit in raising and feeding chickens."

Chicken Resources on the Web

http://www.ithaca.edu/staff/jhenderson/chooks/chlinks.html

John R. Henderson, a librarian at Ithaca College and a Lodi, New York, hobby farmer, has created the ultimate poultry link Web site. While you're there, click on the ICYouSee Handy Dandy Chicken Chart icon to visit one of the Internet's most informative chicken breed charts.

The City Chicken

http://www.thecitychicken.com

Visit The City Chicken to learn how to keep chickens in an urban or suburban setting. Most of the information applies to country-based chicken keeping, too. Don't miss The City Chicken's photo gallery of more than eighty homemade chicken tractors!

FOWL PLAY

http://www.chickens.net

This British chicken site is a joy. Chicken history and excerpts from vintage chicken literature share space with how-to and photo features. You can even play Guess That Bird.

THE OFFICIAL DOM_BIRD WEB SITE

http://www.afn.org/~poultry

Visit The DOM_BIRD Home Page where chickens, turkeys, ducks, and waterfowl rule! Subscribe to the huge, friendly e-mail group, check out the Poultry Breed Encyclopedia, and read a collection of interesting articles including "Build 'Matilda'—an Electric Hen for Less Than $10."

ORGANIC POULTRY RESOURCE MANUAL

http://www.iowaagopportunity.org

Visit Iowa State University's Iowa Agricultural Opportunity Web site and click on Resource Manual Organic Chicken to access their online Poultry Resource Manual. It's a good one.

EGGBID

http://www.eggbid.com

It's the eBay of the poultry world—check it out!

FEATHERSITE

http://www.feathersite.com

Don't miss Feathersite—it's amazing! Links lead to every conceivable poultry topic, organization, and business on the Web.

HOUSECHICKENS

http://groups.yahoo.com/group/housechickens

If you keep pet chickens—in or out of your home—subscribe to housechickens, the friendliest and most fascinating of Yahoo's free chicken-related YahooGroups e-mail lists. Most of the fine folks who contributed tips to the book in your hands are housechickens regulars. Check it out!

MERCK VETERINARY MANUAL

http://www.merckvetmanual.com/mvm/index.jsp

The online version of the Merck Veterinary Manual encompasses more than twelve thousand topics and one thousand illustrations searchable by topic, species, specialty, disease, and keyword. Access is free, compliments of Merck, Inc.

PASTURED POULTRY LINKS AT THE AGRICULTURAL MARKETING RESOURCE CENTER/AGMRC

http://www.agmrc.org/poultry/pasturedmain.html

The Agricultural Marketing Resource Center hosts a collection of links to publications and sites devoted to pastured, free-range, and organic poultry marketing and production.

POULTRY HEALTH ARTICLES AT SHAGBARK BANTAMS

http://shagbarkbantams.com/contents.htm

Most of these easy-to-understand health articles were written by Shagbark

Bantams owner K.J. Theodore and previously appeared in the *Poultry Press*. "Stress" and "Hatching" are especially useful. Folks who love their chickens are sure to appreciate "The Emotional Side of Raising Poultry."

POULTRYHELP

http://www.rockingtranch.com

Four hundred pages of poultry information gathered and posted by the good folks at the Rocking T Ranch and Poultry Farm—that's PoultryHelp. If it's about chickens, it's there.

STATE VETERINARIAN LOCATOR

http://doacs.state.fl.us/ai/statevet.htm

Come to this site to locate State Veterinarians in the United States, Guam, Puerto Rico & U.S. Virgin Islands, including their phone and fax numbers and e-mail addresses.

UNITED STATES ANIMAL HEALTH ASSOCIATION POULTRY PAGE

http://www.usaha.org/species/avian.html

The USAHA provides scores of links to reliable information on every major chicken ailment.

SUGGESTED READINGS

The following books and periodicals were written for small-scale chicken keepers rather than large-scale meat and egg producers. Most are currently in print; the rest are available through out-of-print booksellers or eBay.

BOOKS

Beck-Chenoweth, Herman. *Free-Range Poultry Production, Processing, and Marketing*. Hartshorn, Mo: Back Forty Books, 1997.

This information-packed volume is the definitive work on developing a free-range poultry business. It's a complete how-to incorporating construction plans, feed formulas, slaughter information, and marketing solutions. A companion video is available. Buy them (along with a plethora of other poultry titles) at http://www.back40books.com, (866) 596-9982.

Damerow, Gail. *The Chicken Health*. North Adams, Mass: Storey, 1994.

If you own chickens, you need *The Chicken Health Handbook*. Virtually everything you need to know about evaluating flock health and treating your chickens' parasites, ailments, and injuries; incubating and brooding chicks; nutrition; and anatomy. Even postmortem examinations is presented in easy to comprehend lay terms and packed into this surprisingly inexpensive, 352-page book. The diagnostic guides in this book are outstanding!

———. *A Guide to Raising Chickens: Care, Feeding, Facilities*. North Adams, Mass: Storey, 1995.

Gail Damerow knows her chickens. Whether you keep laying hens or raise meat for the freezer, and no matter your level of expertise, A Guide to Raising

Chickens is a book you'll refer to time and time again.

————. *Your Chickens; A Kid's Guide to Raising and Showing*. North Adams, Mass: Story, 1993.
It would be easy to say *Your Chickens is A Guide to Raising Chickens* rewritten for kids, but it's so much more. Great pictures and line drawings, interesting layouts, and lively writing make this a terrific introductory book for chicken lovers of all ages.

Feldman, Thea. *Who You Callin' Chicken?* New York: Harry N Abrams, 2003.
Written for kids ages 4 to 8, but fun for chicken admirers of all age, this zany volume spotlights a wide variety of plain and fancy chicken breeds, examining their feathers, life cycle, evolution and more. Fowl photographer Stephen Green-Armytage's fantastic chicken photos are a sheer delight.

Feltwell, Ray. *Small-Scale Poultry-Keeping; A Guide to Free-range Poultry Production*. London: Faber & Faber, 2002.
In Britain, backyard hen keeping is a long-standing tradition. Everything from do-it-yourself small-scale poultry housing to feeding, health, and breeding is covered in this cleverly written 196-page handbook.

Gloss, Karma E. *"Remedies for Health Problems of the Organic Laying Flock: A Compendium and Workbook of Management, Nutrition, Herbal and Homeopathic Remedies,"* http://kingbird-farm.com (accessed October 27, 2004).
This 60-page guide to treating chickens using homeopathic, herbal, and other holistic remedies was made possible by a grant from the Sustainable Agriculture Research and Education Project (SARE). An inexpensive print version is available from the author at (607) 657-2860 or karma@kingbird-farm.com. The complete text is downloadable as a free PDF file at http://kingbirdfarm.com.

Green-Armytage, Stephen. *Extraordinary Chickens*. New York: Harry L Abrams, 2000.
Exotic show chickens of all sizes, shapes, and colors parade through these pages in 165 photos, each the work of *Life* magazine photographer, Stephen Green-Armytage. Fifty breeds are lavishly pictured and described.

Hams, Fred. *Old Poultry Breeds*. Buckinghamshire, UK: Shire Books, 2000.
Old Poultry Breeds (like all the revised Shire Books) packs more information into forty pages than most books four times its size! Pictures (one hundred of them, fifty-two in color) and history are its strong points; most every breed we know in America (and a lot we don't) are covered in this neat, small volume.

Kilarski, Barbara. *Keep Chickens! Tending Small Flocks in Cities, Suburbs, and Other Small Places*. North Adams, Mass: Storey, 2003.
Urban chickens are the rage. In this 150-page guidebook, author Barbara Kilarski

tells all—from determining if chickens are legal in your city or suburb, to locating and raising chicks, to feeding and housing them. The text is peppered with poultry facts and stories about the author's three hens. This gentle, fun and informative volume is (except for this one) my favorite chicken book of all time.

Lee, Andy and Pat Foreman. *Chicken Tractor: The Permaculture Guide to Happy Hens and Healthy Soil.*
Good Earth Publishing, 1998.
This is the book that started the chicken tractor phenomenon. While inspirational, instructions for building the actual tractor are somewhat sketchy, so read the book to understand the concept, then adapt the author's design or use one of many online chicken tractor plans. Your garden and your chickens will love you if you do!

Rossier, Jay. *Living with Chickens: Everything You Need to Know to Raise Your Own Backyard Flock.*
Guilford, Conn.: Lyons Press, 2002.
Detailed how-to advice on housing, hatching, buying, feeding, and butchering combined with dozens of detailed illustrations and outstanding photography make this an especially appealing introduction to small-scale chicken keeping.

Percy, Pam. *The Complete Chicken: An Entertaining History of Chickens.*
Stillwater, Minn.: Voyageur Press, 2002.
Chicken history; chicken breeds; the chicken's role in art and pop culture, myth, legend, religion, and folklore; chicken collectibles; a wide selection of words and phrases inspired by chicks, technical poultry terms, and instructions on how crow in different languages and other trivia; vintage art and beautiful photos—they're all tucked between the covers of *The Complete Chicken.*

Salatin, Joel. *Pastured Poultry Profits.* Chelsea Green Publishing Company, 1996. If you dream of operating a profitable pasture-based broiler business, this is your book. Everything from selecting a breed to building pens to marketing the finished—it's here.

Smith, Page and Daniel, Charles. *The Chicken Book.* Athens: University of Georgia Press, 2002.
The Chicken Book is in-depth look at chickens through time and place. It's not light reading, but serious chicken aficionados will love this fat volume of chicken fact, fiction, myth, and folklore. It's fascinating material. Highly recommended.

Staples, Tamara and Velbel, Christa. *The Fairest Fowl; Portraits of Championship Chickens.* San Francisco: Chronicle Books, 2001.
Photographer Tamara Staples brings us thirty-five full-page portraits of fancy show chickens, accompanied by breed information and a fact-filled tour of the show ring.

Thear, Katie. *Free-Range Poultry.* Diamond Farm Books, 2003.

Although this is a British book, most North American free-range poultry producers consider this their business bible. *Free-Range Poultry* covers breeds, housing, feeding, management, eggs, breeding, rearing and recording in 181 pages and seventy-seven color photos.

Vorwald Dohner, Janet. *The Encyclopedia of Historic and Endangered Livestock and Poultry Breeds.* Yale University Press, 2001. This is a handsome volume that discusses in depth the merits of rare breed conservation and profiles nearly two hundred breeds of livestock (goats, sheep, swine, cattle, horses and asses) and poultry (including heirloom chickens).

MAGAZINES

Feather Fancier
http://www.featherfancier.on.ca
(519) 542-6859
featherfancier@ebtech.net
Feather Fancier is "The only Canadian Publication catering to Breeders and Fanciers of Purebred Poultry, Fancy & Racing Pigeons, Domestic & Ornamental Waterfowl, Pheasants and other Avian Species." Published eleven times a year, it's distributed throughout North America and abroad.

Poultry Press
www.poultrypress.com
(765) 827-0932
info@poultrypress.com
Poultry Press' masthead states it's been "Promoting Standard Bred Poultry Since 1914." It's an information-packed monthly and not to be missed. Visit the Web site to peruse sample articles, view a great image gallery featuring fancy fowls, order a sample issue, or subscribe.

Show Bird Journal
http://members.aol.com/showbird62/showbirdjournal.html
(256) 757-1471
showbird62@aol
Show Bird Journal is a small, but growing, monthly devoted to show and fancy chickens and the only one published in full color.

Chicken Stories

SUPER CHICKEN!
PIGGY HERO

About three and one-half years ago, I was living on the family farm in Brooks, Maine, and attended a local country fair, where I fell in love with a fluffy black Silkie rooster who was sitting in a ten-year-old girl's lap, complacently allowing himself to be petted. I went back and forth from that poultry exhibit (always my favorite part of any country fair, followed closely by prize-winning veggies) and finally went home with that roo-boy in a cardboard box.

That roo was Piggy (originally named Suleyman) and since I had only the one, and no chicken house set up, and because I like all manner of living things in my house, he became a very pampered and beloved house pet, and in many ways my very best friend. Piggy has never been constrained in any way, except to the house (though, of course, he does have supervised yard forays) and so has developed his own routines. When he's not asleep, Piggy socializes. Wherever the people are is where he will be, either sitting behind them on the back of the couch watching videos, or nestled on the bed beside a lazy reader, or pattering from room to room as errands are tended to.

But at night, Piggy makes his way to his bed, which is the back of the couch (eternally towel-draped), and, generally speaking, he will then sleep through all manner of activity and noise. Now and then he'll arise with a second wind if the lights are turned on or if he hears activity in a distant room and finds it too quiet where he is, but generally he sticks to his routine. In the morning, he hops up, crows, gets himself a bite to eat, and seeks out a bed to jump into, where he will greet any sign of movement by gently nibbling noses or tugging on hair in an attempt to waken a sleeper for a petting session. If he is unsuccessful in his attempts, as he often is, he will settle down to nap quietly until his companions finally arise. Often, I have walked by my significant other's room to see a heap of bedclothes, with nothing emerging but Piggy's rotund rump and a rather limp hand petting said rump.

One night, Mark was away, and our housemate Paul and I were the only humans in the house. Piggy had gone to bed as usual several hours before, and Paul had retired to his upstairs bedroom. I was in my room at the back of the house, picking sluggishly at a couple watercolor commissions. Around 11:30, I passed Piggy on the way to the kitchen to put on the tea kettle, but Piggy never woke up, although I briefly rubbed his back in passing, as always.

It can't have been two minutes later that I heard Piggy hit the floor with a thud. This caught my attention, because it was late and there was no conversation for him to be seeking out, no lights, nothing to wake him. I called his name. Suddenly he rushed into my room and leapt onto the bed, clearly agitated and making distress noises. Thinking vaguely that perhaps an animal had gotten in and frightened him, I ran through the living room to find the kitchen half engulfed in flames, visible only as a large red glow through thick black smoke. I tried to turn on the light, and thought the bulb must have blown.

(I later discovered that it was still working, but the smoke was so thick was the smoke that I could not tell if it was on or off.) I screamed for Paul and fumbled with the outside door until it opened, got the outside light on and tore open the door of the bulkhead to the basement, where the garden hose had recently been stored. As Paul dialed 911, I turned the on hose full force, aiming it at the door of the kitchen as smoke pumped out like a huge black caterpillar. By the time the fire trucks arrived, the walls and ceiling were still smoldering, but I had gotten the flames out some minutes before. We were hustled from the house and the fire axes went to work. At one point, I sneaked in and checked on Piggy, and he was standing alertly on the bed where I last saw him, so I left him there and went back outside while the firemen finished up. They said that surely, after another minute, we would have lost the whole house and– they did not need to sayit – possibly our lives as well. They asked what had happened and I told them all, including Piggy's role. As they were winding down, I was standing in the smoldering remains of my kitchen, talking to two firemen in full gear, when one of them cried, "There's the chicken!" Piggy, hearing my voice, had taken that for an all- clear, and left the refuge of my bed to amble out, rather timidly by his own standards, to be introduced.

The next evening, Piggy, who when he is not being a hero is just a regular stay-at-home kind of guy, ate a prodigious

quantity of his favorite food–a peanut butter, cream cheese and olive sandwich (you read right)– wiped his beak repeatedly on my leg, and snuggled down beside me for a nap. I intend to propose that a monument be erected in Piggy's likeness on the fire station lawn!
–*Cindy Ryan*

Cindy Ryan is a School of Visual Arts (NYC)-trained artist and children's writer. Her wonderful animal-themed artwork can be viewed at tinyurl.com/bt2y. Cindy specializes in custom animal portraits marketed via eBay; her eBay user name is lajete. For further information, contact Cindy at: cinbud@acadia.net

PUNKY RAINBOW
Spring 2001-March 26, 2003
Member of the Kroll Family

Love with Wings for $1.25
There was something about her.
When she came home she followed me everywhere.
Punky Rainbow became a house chicken for a while.
She would sing and follow me around the house.
Punky kept her little wings outstretched like
preparing for take off as she and our family
played tag up and down the hallway.
We trusted each other completely.
She was so gentle.
I could pick her up without a single flap.
Punky Rainbow would preen my eye lashes.
Many city folk met her at our pet store;
Punky was the first living chicken they had ever seen.
When she moved to the farm to have babies,
Punky and I still sat and talked.
She seemed to understand what I said,
and chirped and purred back to me.
She went with us camping, to the beach,
sledding, and to the pet store.
"Just this side of Heaven is a place called the Rainbow Bridge where Punky
Rainbow is playing. We'll cross the Rainbow Bridge together."

–*Jennifer Kroll, Fluff 'N Strut Silkies*

A Tribute to Eggnus (2003–2004)

Eggnus came into our lives on April 6, 2003. I had placed an order for two chicks at a feed store and when we picked them up, I saw a box labeled White Rocks. Inside it were the cutest yellow chicks with a touch of peach on their chests! One chick looked up at me, almost pleading for me to pick her. I couldn't resist; I had found my Eggnus.

I had a Silkie hen named Emma, who was raising two chicks of her own, and Emma adopted Eggnus, who immediately cuddled under Emma and joined the other chicks. All through Eggnus' life, she remained close to her foster mom.

However, Eggnus quickly outgrew her mom and the other large breed chicks. She would trail behind the others and when she'd run we called it the "wiggle waddle." She would hop back and forth sideways and she had trouble stopping once she started running; once she even knocked down a rooster who was standing in her path!

When she was four months old, Eggnus went lame. I took her to a vet. Eggnus was the talk of the waiting room-this big white chicken in a dog crate. She made friends with everyone at the vet's office, including the vet's assistant, who told me Eggnus was a Cornish/Rock cross.

The vet thought Eggnus had injured her back jumping down out of the coop because she was obese. At four months, she weighed over nine pounds! She was given vitamin shots and medicine and I put her on a diet.

After that, Eggnus would go outside in the mornings with the flock, then she'd come in the house where she had her own personal fan. She lived in a plastic crate in the hallway. She'd flash those big eyes at you and tilt her head sideways. She loved to be petted and greeted everyone who passed by.

Eggnus never regained her ability to walk any long distances. She would take a couple of steps, then she would lie down. But that never stopped her from trying. Eggnus was determined to walk.

Eggnus died January 3, 2004, in her sleep. I knew from the research I did on her breed that she wouldn't live to be very old. However, knowing this didn't make her passing any easier. We buried her beside a peony bush she had loved to lie beneath.

She always had a cheerful attitude and the sweetest personality. I knew Eggnus was special the first time I saw her—I just didn't know how special she really was. I will never know why a Cornish/Rock cross was in a box with the White Rock chicks but if she hadn't been, I would never have known my Eggnus. I have no regrets. If I had known what I know now, I would do it all over again.

A gentle giant of a chicken with a heart of gold: Eggnus, I will love and remember you always.

—*Patty Mousty*

Photo Credits

The sources for the photographs that appear in this volume are listed below. Sources are listed by chapter in order of appearance.

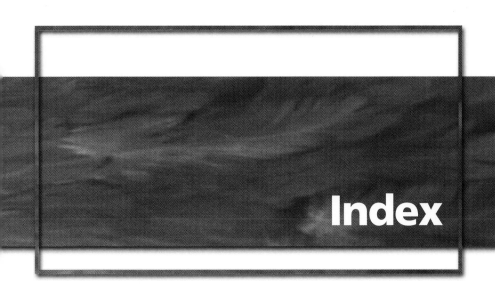

Index

ABOUT THE AUTHOR

Sue Weaver has written hundreds of articles about animals over the years, is a contributing editor of *Hobby Farms* magazine, and is the author of *Sheep: Small-Scale Sheep Keeping for Pleasure and Profit*. Sue maintains a flock of chickens that includes Barred Rock Cochins, a Silver-Laced Wyandotte, a larger brown Cochin, a Red Jungle Fowl, and an assortment of barnies. She also breeds Keyrrey - Shee miniature sheep, American Curly horses, and AMHR miniature horses of the cob type. Sue lives in Mammoth Spring, Arkansas.